To:

From:

100 Favorite

BIBLE VERSES

COUNTRYMAN ®

A Division of Thomas Nelson Publishers

THOMAS NELSON
Since 1798

100 Favorite Bible Verses

© 2017 by Thomas Nelson

Published in Nashville, Tennessee, by Thomas Nelson. Thomas Nelson is a registered trademark of HarperCollins Christian Publishing, Inc.

Interior Illustrations: CreativeToons, Iuliia Zubkova, LarysaZabrotskaya, and Lizamperini of Creative Market

Thomas Nelson titles may be purchased in bulk for educational, business, fund-raising, or sales promotional use. For information, please e-mail SpecialMarkets@ThomasNelson.com.

ISBN-13: 978-0-7180-9695-3

Printed in China

17 18 19 20 21 TIMS 6 5 4 3 2 1

CONTENTS

CONTENTS

CONTENTS

CONTENTS

CONTENTS

CONTENTS

CONTENTS

CONTENTS

CONTENTS

CONTENTS

INTRODUCTION

Favorite Bible Verses

Your word is a lamp to my feet
and a light to my path.

Psalm 119:105

What is your favorite verse in the Bible? Simply trying to answer that question helps you appreciate both the life-giving power of God's Word and the significant role it has played in your life. How can you possibly choose only one verse—or only five, for that matter?

To compile this collection, we asked people to share the Bible verses they cherished the most. Responses flooded in from all over the world. One thing was certain for all who responded—God's Word had touched each of their lives in a way that was inspired and deeply personal. One wrote that a passage from the Psalms had spoken words of comfort when she was feeling alone. For another, a parable of Jesus had inspired him to pray as he'd never prayed

before. Each person had a unique story to tell about a verse that had changed his or her life.

Scripture truly is living and active (Hebrews 4:12), speaking to us in different ways at different times. God uses His Word to guide us in times of doubt and sustain us in times of loss. His words become a rich tool as we pray Scripture back to its author, and He enables us to remember specific passages so we can comfort others and share His life-changing truth. The Bible teaches us not only how to live but also why we live—and it reminds us that God's love is the focal point of life.

So what is *your* favorite verse? When you hear that question, your current favorite may come to mind right away. Or your first thought could be a life verse

you chose when you named Jesus as your Savior and Lord. Maybe your parents shared one of their favorite passages with you as a child, and it has remained in your heart.

Or perhaps life is difficult right now, and you have recently discovered a verse that you know the Lord handpicked just for you for just this time. Or maybe a particular verse had a significant impact on you at a different point in your life, and those words will always be incredibly meaningful to you.

In the pages that follow, you'll find some of your own favorite verses and perhaps some new favorites as well. If you'd like, use the final pages to add more favorites to the collection. You'll find that each passage

offers its own gifts of comfort, direction, hope, and inspiration.

Enjoy this tangible reminder of the treasures that await you in God's Word. May this devotional grow your appreciation for Scripture and fuel your passion to read it, know it, and live it.

LOVE IS . . .

*M*aybe you've heard it suggested that as you read these verses from 1 Corinthians 13, you should replace the words *love* and *it* with your own name. That can be a very convicting exercise as we realize how far short of God's standards we fall.

Here is another option: Think of this passage as a description of God's love for you. Let His words heal you, encourage you, and guide you. Let them reinforce the truth that nothing will ever separate you from His love (Romans 8:38–39) and that He will never leave you (Matthew 28:20).

After basking in God's love, ask Him whom He would like you to love today. He may bring to mind someone you need to forgive (because love "keeps no record of being wronged"), He may prompt you to pray about a coworker you tend to avoid (because love is "patient"), or He may nudge you to take brownies to the new neighbors or a meal to a grieving family (because love is "kind"). Listen for God's direction, do what He says, and enjoy the blessing that comes with obeying Him and loving others with His love.

Thank You, Lord, that You are love and You never give up on us. Please use me to share Your love with others.

1 Corinthians 13:4–7 NLT

Love is *patient* and *kind*. Love
is not jealous or boastful or proud
or rude. It does not demand
its own way. It is not irritable,
and it keeps no record of being
wronged. It does not rejoice about
injustice but *rejoices* whenever
the truth wins out. Love never
gives up, never loses *faith*, is
always *hopeful*, and endures
through every circumstance.

STRONG AND COURAGEOUS

*N*othing in your life surprises God. Every event, every conversation, every joy, and every sorrow—He has either planned or allowed all these. He knows that life on this planet will mean trials, pain, heartache, and challenges.

After Moses' death Joshua faced an overwhelming challenge; he had enormous shoes to fill when he stepped up to lead Israel. The Almighty knew that Joshua would have occasion to feel weak, overwhelmed, and discouraged. He also knew that Joshua had legitimate reasons to fear and be dismayed. And God spoke to those needs, which are your needs as well: "Be strong and of good courage; do not be afraid, nor be dismayed."

But God didn't stop there for Joshua—and He doesn't stop there for you. He gives you an empowering reason why you needn't fear or be discouraged: "For the LORD your God is with you wherever you go."

So whenever you face something that makes you feel anything but strong and courageous, remind yourself that God is with you. And put one foot in front of the other one more time.

Thank You, Lord, for being with me wherever I go. With You as my source of strength and encouragement, I can face any challenge.

Joshua 1:9

"Have I not commanded you? Be **strong** and of good *courage*; do not be afraid, nor be dismayed, for the Lord your *God* is with you wherever you go."

9

THE GOOD SHEPHERD

*D*o you know how similar human beings and sheep are? You may think of picturesque animals grazing on a gentle hillside, but it's not always such a pretty picture! Sheep have a herd mentality; they'll follow their mob even into danger. They can be fearful and ornery and find themselves in all kinds of messes.

Although we might not choose that kind of company, Jesus graciously does. He is our Good Shepherd, going where others would never go to pull us out of sin. Why? Because He loves us for who He made us to be—even with our sheeplike ways.

The cross is the supreme example of Jesus sparing no cost for His sheep who were lost in sin. Yet Jesus' shepherding didn't stop on Calvary. Read again the promises in Psalm 23:1–3, 6. What provision are you most in need of today? What words offer you hope?

Thank your Good Shepherd for His sweet, devoted care for you. Ask forgiveness for the ways you fall into step with the world's flock rather than sticking with the Shepherd. Then close with praise for the "goodness and mercy" that, by God's grace, will follow you all the days of your life.

Lord, help me walk along Your paths all my days.

Psalm 23:1–3, 6

The LORD is my *shepherd*; I shall not want. He makes me to lie down in green pastures; He leads me beside the still waters. He *restores* my soul; He leads me in the paths of righteousness for His name's sake. . . . Surely *goodness* and *mercy* shall follow me all the days of my life; and I will dwell in the house of the LORD *forever*.

THE CURE

*H*ave you ever felt that something was inherently wrong with the world? With you? If life feels broken, if the bad seems to overtake the good, if you just keep messing things up—you've noticed something crucial about reality. Our hearts are sick with sin, and the world is too. As the prophet Jeremiah said, "The heart is more deceitful than all else and is desperately sick; who can understand it?" (Jeremiah 17:9 NASB).

But there is a cure for the sickness of our sins! The apostle John reveals this life-giving truth: when we confess our sins, God forgives and heals us—and His forgiveness is not some cold, sterile treatment. It was made possible by an act of immeasurable and costly love: His sinless Son dying on the cross as payment for our sins—to heal us and to cleanse us. God removes our sins from us "as far as the east is from the west" (Psalm 103:12), and He washes us "whiter than snow" (Psalm 51:7).

Yes, there's something wrong with us: we are sinners. But because of Jesus' sacrifice on the cross, our Savior graciously forgives us and heals our souls.

Jesus, I joyfully accept Your amazing grace that makes me whole!

1 John 1:9

If we confess
our sins, He
is *faithful* and
just to *forgive* us
our sins and to
cleanse us from all
unrighteousness.

JUSTICE, MERCY, HUMILITY

*S*uppose you have to verbally explain to a child how to tie a shoe. It wouldn't be easy, would it? "Make bunny ears" wouldn't have much meaning to a shoe-tying novice. Sometimes showing, not merely telling, is a much more effective way of teaching.

God used this approach when He sent His Son to show us—in person—what is good: justice, mercy, and humility. Jesus overturned the tables of the money changers who had made His Father's house a den of thieves. He spoke out against the Jewish religious leaders who used their power for their own good. Jesus always does what is just.

Jesus healed the sick, the blind, and the lame. He reached out to those who were rejected in society—the Samaritans, prostitutes, and tax collectors—all sinners like you and me. Jesus loves mercy.

Jesus submitted to God's will by giving His life for us. When soldiers arrested Him, Jesus could have called down the angels to help Him, but He did His Father's will so that the Scriptures would be fulfilled. Jesus always walks humbly with God.

May we live out what Christ has shown us to do.

Lord, help me to do justly, to love mercy,
and to walk humbly with You.

Micah 6:8

He has shown you,
O man, what is *good*;
and what does the
Lord require of you
but to do *justly*,
to love *mercy*,
and to walk *humbly*
with your God?

THE GREATEST COMMANDS

*L*ove God with all you are and love your neighbor just as you love yourself. These two greatest commands are simple enough to understand. Living them out, though, is an entirely different matter—and the second command is especially difficult if you don't find it easy to love yourself.

Loving ourselves can be tough. We tend to judge ourselves based on the world's idea of what is lovable, and that's often unattainable. But God is concerned with what's in our hearts, not how we look or what we do. If we look at ourselves from His point of view—as saved and precious—we might find it easier to love ourselves.

So spend time reading God's Word. It's been called His love letter to humanity. As you read and fill up with His love, you'll find that you can love God in so many ways— with your heart, soul, strength, and mind. And when you focus on loving God, you'll naturally spend time loving those around you. A relationship with God always leads to love—a love so strong that you can love yourself and others with His love.

Lord, may Your love transform me and free me to love myself, to love others better, and to love You with more of myself.

Luke 10:27

"'You shall *love* the
Lord your God with
all your *heart*, with all
your *soul*, with all your
strength, and with all
your *mind*' and
'your neighbor
as yourself.'"

GOD'S GREAT GIFT

John 3:16 may be the most widely known and most frequently memorized verse in the Bible. But our familiarity with these words can cause us to miss their vital message. Let's try to look at the words as if for the first time.

"God so loved the world" that He chose to show His love with an action that became the focal point of history. God gave His "only begotten Son" to the very people who had rejected His ways and instead lived however they saw fit. This undeserved gift required immeasurable sacrifice from both God the Father and God the Son. The Father gave His sinless Son to suffer on our behalf. The Son would not only go to the cross, but He would also experience complete separation from His Father.

But after three days Jesus rose from the dead, demonstrating His power over sin and death. And whoever believes in the resurrected Christ will not die but will have "everlasting life." Everlasting life! That joyful communion with God the Father and God the Son will last throughout eternity.

Father, keep my eyes focused on Jesus, my heart overflowing with love for You, and my lips ready to share the good news of Your love.

John 3:16 KJV

"For God so *loved* the world, that he *gave* his only begotten Son, that whosoever *believeth* in him should not perish, but have everlasting *life*."

BRING BACK LOYALTY

L *oyalty.* That word may sound as if it needs to be dusted off. We can all think of stories depicting loyal knights and subjects, of characters fiercely loyal to a mission or cause, but today loyalty can seem the stuff of legend. Maybe a diehard fan will cheer on the same team for a lifetime despite wins or losses, but to what else—if anything—are we as loyal?

In today's verse we see Ruth making a shockingly strong statement of loyalty. She declares her loyalty to her mother-in-law, Naomi. She is willing to travel to Naomi's land and to settle among Naomi's people. Most striking, though, is her pledge to follow Naomi's God. Ruth chose to forsake all she had known growing up in Moab; she chose to follow the God of Israel. Ruth declared her loyalty to Him with her words and her actions.

Today you may have opportunities to declare your loyalty to God with your words and actions. Do so bravely, knowing that your faithful God will empower you. You may waver in your loyalty to Him, but know that His loyalty and faithfulness to you will never fade.

Lord, I choose to be like Ruth and stay loyal to the people in my life—and most of all, to You.

Ruth 1:16

Entreat me not to leave you, or to turn back from *following* after you; for wherever you go, I will go; and wherever you lodge, I will *lodge*; your people shall be my people, and your God, my *God*.

GOOD DIRECTIONS

Think about the time it takes to enter a destination into your GPS or maps app on your phone. It's only a moment, right? We all know that the time we spend seeking directions is probably only a fraction of the time it might take us to get to our destination without any directions at all.

This same principle holds true in life. God will give us directions, but we need to take time to listen: to read His Word and spend time in prayer. We may think we are too busy for these things, but God turns that logic on its head. When we spend time with God, we find that we are able to do more through His strength.

Do you believe this truth? Perhaps you've been enjoying an intimate relationship with your heavenly Father. Or perhaps you've never believed this truth enough to take a step of faith. If that's the case, what do you have to lose? Make time with your Lord a priority, watch Him bless the rest of your day, and learn anew that you can take God at His word. God will teach you and guide you through each day!

*Lord God, help me make the time to listen
for Your instructions and enable me to
travel according to Your directions.*

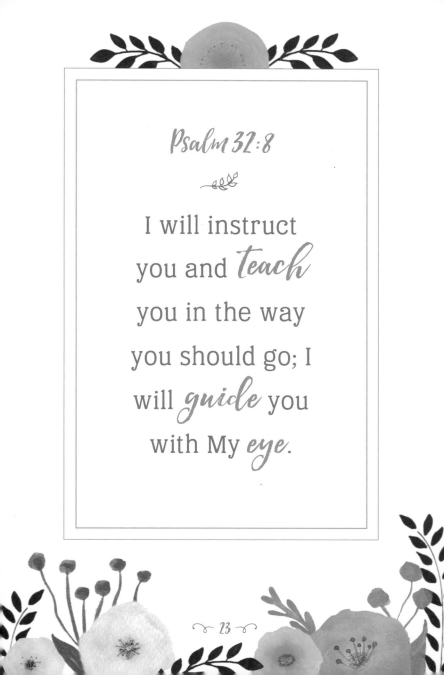

Psalm 32:8

I will instruct
you and *teach*
you in the way
you should go; I
will *guide* you
with My *eye*.

A LIFESTYLE OF PRAYER

*I*t's a command that comes with a promise. *Pray.* Pray about everything. Pray with thanksgiving. Pray all the time. But this command is not a burden. Being able to talk to the almighty Creator of the universe—anytime, anywhere—is a mind-boggling privilege! Try an experiment: start your morning with prayer and continue throughout the day. Put it in your calendar, make a point to do it at meals, and lift up a short word of prayer before every new project, event, or task. Pray for your own needs, and also ask God to intervene in the lives of those around you. As you add everyday communion with God to your lifestyle, what does it do to your anxiety level?

Paul knew that prayer also means trading anxiety for God's peace. The apostle faced many dangers and had plenty of reasons to worry, but he practiced what he preached. He prayed and knew unshakable, incomprehensible, divine peace. You can know it too. Today, trade worry for "the peace of God, which surpasses all understanding."

Prayer is an amazing privilege, Lord.
Show me how to pray always and about
everything, and to do so with thanksgiving.

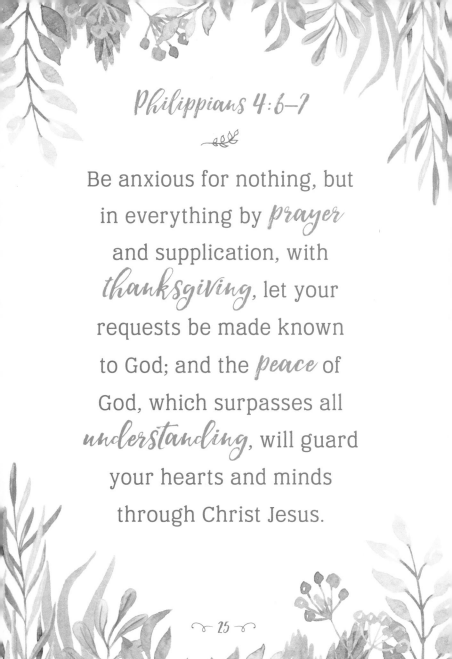

Philippians 4:6–7

Be anxious for nothing, but in everything by *prayer* and supplication, with *thanksgiving*, let your requests be made known to God; and the *peace* of God, which surpasses all *understanding*, will guard your hearts and minds through Christ Jesus.

WINGS LIKE EAGLES

*T*hink of the iconic image of an eagle soaring on the breeze. Did you know that eagles have a seven-foot wingspan and are able to carry well over their body weight? With incredible strength and speed, they can appear to be motionless in hurricane-force winds. And as they soar and dive, they appear to do so effortlessly.

With these facts in mind, consider the promise in Isaiah 40:31 that you "shall mount up with wings like eagles." Yes, you will grow weary as you journey through life, but you don't have to stay at that low point. Turn to God; wait on Him. Open His Word and remind yourself of His strength, power, and love. Let God know what He already knows, that you are feeling overwhelmed. Let Him lift you up.

One more eagle fact: in contrast to some birds, the eagle is never left incapacitated during molting, when all its feathers are replaced each year. Similarly, as you wait upon the Lord, you will find yourself replenished and renewed inside and out. As you rest in His strength, you will find your hopelessness replaced by hope, your weariness by energy, and your fear by courage.

God, thank You for drawing near to me when I am in need of the renewal only You can give.

Isaiah 40:31

Those who wait on
the LORD shall renew
their *strength*; they
shall mount up with
wings like *eagles*,
they shall run and not
be weary, they shall
walk and not faint.

REVEALING WORD

*S*ome things that hurt us can actually be good for us. Getting a flu shot, setting a broken bone, hearing the truth about where we are messing up—hurts like these are, in the long run, good for us.

God's Word is that kind of tool if we let it be: it can hurt us in order to heal us and grow us. Understanding that, the author of Hebrews described Scripture as "sharper than any two-edged sword." The author was aware that, as Scripture pierces our hearts, God's Word reveals the sinful thoughts, motives, and desires that reside there. It uncovers our innermost hearts, and it invites us to open ourselves to God with piercing honesty and vulnerability.

Yes, God's Word reveals to us our sin, and that's never a pretty picture. But seeing our sin clearly is key to confessing it, receiving forgiveness for it, and being delivered from its hold on us. God has designed His living and active Word to be a truth-revealing tool, showing us exactly what we need in order to be more like Christ.

Teach me, Lord, to be open to Your transforming work and willing to be hurt by Your truth in order to become more like Your Son.

Hebrews 4:12 ESV

The word of God is *living*
and *active*, sharper than
any two-edged sword,
piercing to the division
of *soul* and of *spirit*, of
joints and of marrow, and
discerning the thoughts and
intentions of the *heart*.

BEYOND THE IMPOSSIBLE

*M*ary was a young girl when she received an amazing promise. She was going about her day when suddenly the angel Gabriel appeared. As if his appearance weren't surprising enough, his announcement made his remarkable presence pale in comparison. *She* was favored by the Lord? *She* was blessed among women? She, who had never been with a man, would conceive a son? And had Gabriel really said to call this miracle baby "the Son of God" (Luke 1:35)? The answer to these questions was yes, for "with God nothing will be impossible."

What situation in your life seems impossible? What relationship, what state of your heart, what physical circumstances seem beyond repair and even beyond hope? Do you need to find a job? Have you been praying that someone you love will walk with the Lord? Are you asking the Lord to renew the passion in your marriage?

Keep calling out to the One for whom nothing is impossible. He is the powerful God of redemption, the One who calls you His child and who cares for you. He hears your prayers, and He will act.

Lord, I ask You to work in these difficult situations in my life for the good of those involved and for Your glory.

Luke 1:37

"With God
nothing
will be
impossible."

WHAT DO YOU TREASURE?

*Y*ou can probably name someone you know who is climbing up the ladder of success and pursuing the latest technology, the most luxurious car, the finest gated community, and the most elite schools for their children. It's easy to judge, but maybe we're not so different. What stuff are you holding on to with a death grip? What do you think is valuable?

Think about what God means by "treasures in heaven." God's treasure is what He finds valuable. Ephesians tells us that He is "rich in mercy, because of His great love" (2:4). So it stands to reason that in God's economy, riches come in the form of grace, mercy, and love rather than stock dividends, designer clothes, and expensive trips.

How can we value what He values? Value people, who "were not redeemed with corruptible things, like silver or gold . . . but with the precious blood of Christ" (1 Peter 1:18–19). Build up a heavenly bank account with love for His people: forgiveness given, grace extended, warm hugs, tender looks, heartfelt contentment, joy, and love.

How healthy is your heavenly bank account? And when will you make your next deposit?

*Father God, teach me to value what
is valuable to You. Help me recognize
opportunities to lay up treasures in heaven.*

Matthew 6:20–21

"Lay up for yourselves *treasures* in *heaven*, where neither moth nor rust destroys and where thieves do not break in and steal. For where your treasure is, there your *heart* will be also."

SOMETHING FROM NOTHING

*W*hen we create, we use what has already been created. An artist works with stone, paint, canvas, or charcoals. A builder works with concrete, wood, and glass. A chef works with fine ingredients.

When God began creating everything that exists, He didn't have a stock of supplies to use. He created something—countless somethings—out of absolutely nothing. He didn't have a palette of atoms, molecules, cells, or DNA to choose from. He was on His own—and the amazing creation that we know was the result.

The first step in God's creative process was the creation of light. According to Genesis, "In the beginning God created the heavens and the earth. The earth was without form, and void; and darkness was on the face of the deep" (1:1–2). Then God commanded, "Let there be light," and it was so.

Truly, nothing is impossible for God—and what a comforting truth. He can make something of the nothing that you may feel your life has become. Submit to Him as did the "darkness . . . on the face of the deep," and see what our powerful and creative God does.

"Let there be light." May those words keep me mindful of Your power, Lord, as I face situations that seem impossible to me.

Genesis 1:3

Then *God* said,
"Let there be light";
and there
was *light*.

IN HIS ARMS

*D*epending on a person's build, there's a distance of about fourteen inches between the brain and the heart. That distance might as well be ten thousand miles sometimes.

We can know a lot of theology. We can read the Bible and point to passages that describe His power and His mercy. We can quote scriptures about God's love. But are we able to feel God's love in our hearts? Do we believe that God truly is all powerful and ever merciful? Does our faith extend from head knowledge to experiential heart knowledge?

Building a bridge between head and heart is especially difficult when we're suffering. Our hurting hearts ask, "Why, God?" But perhaps what we need is not an answer—it's not head knowledge of why we are suffering. We need heart knowledge of how much our Father loves us, to know that He is in control and that He will make "all things work together for good" (Romans 8:28).

Isaiah tells us God will gather us into His arms. So when you are in pain, fall into those loving arms, knowing with both head and heart that He will carry you through.

*Lord, I thank You for giving Yourself when I
need comfort that words can't communicate.*

Isaiah 40:11

He will feed His flock
like a *shepherd*;
He will gather the
lambs with His arm,
and *carry* them
in His bosom, and
gently *lead* those
who are with young.

SONG OF FAITHFULNESS

"*G*ive thanks to the Lord, for he is good; his love endures forever" (Psalm 118:1 NIV). This joyful note opens Psalm 118, and the joy continues as the psalmist celebrates God's faithfulness to him through the years.

Now consider God's great faithfulness to you over the span of your lifetime. Think first about your own story and how God brought you to faith in Jesus.

Using the Bible as a pattern for praise, follow the psalmist's path through Psalm 118, verse by verse. Think of times of distress in your life. When have you called on God and experienced Him taking you to "a spacious place" where you could feel safe (v. 5 NIV)?

Overflowing with gratitude, the psalmist vowed to "proclaim what the Lord has done" (v. 17 NIV). How can you do the same? When has the Lord "chastened [you] severely" (v. 18 NIV), and what good did God bring out of that experience?

Near the end of the song, the psalmist proclaimed, "You are my God, and I will praise you" (v. 28 NIV). The joyous tone is unmistakable. Like the psalmist, let that joy in the Lord and gratitude to Him be unmistakable in your words, attitudes, and actions today.

*Lord, help me always to be conscious of
these reasons for joy and gratitude.*

Psalm 118:5 NIV

When hard
pressed, I cried
to the *LORD*;
he brought me into
a *spacious* place.

EFFECTIVE PRAYER

We go through dry seasons when God seems distant and prayer seems pointless, so we skip it altogether. We may also enter a season of great pain and devastating loss when we simply can't pray, and we rely on the prayers of our sisters and brothers in Christ. Then come those prayer times when God seems to be in the same room with us as we pray and when God responds in ways far greater than we would have ever imagined. We enter our times of prayer with great anticipation that God will work mightily in our lives.

In between these extreme experiences, we keep up with regular prayer times—those acts of obedience that we do out of love for our Lord. We pray because He calls us to; we pray because we love Him.

James reminds us that, by God's grace, our prayers can and will avail much. We are privileged to be adopted into God's family, and as His children we always have the opportunity to talk with Him. As you devote yourself to this discipline, thank God for the power He brings through prayer, and watch Him act!

God, please keep me disciplined and expectant as I make prayer a part of my life.

James 5:16

The effective,
fervent
prayer of a
righteous
man
avails much.

STRENGTH IN WEAKNESS

*T*he apostle Paul told the Corinthians about a weakness he struggled with. He didn't specifically state what his struggle entailed, and perhaps it simply didn't matter. After all, the truth Paul was teaching is relevant to everyone.

And what was that truth? The apostle had learned that Jesus' grace was all he needed, whatever life's demands. The risen Lord Himself had told Paul, "My grace is sufficient for you, for my power is made perfect in weakness." Paul, therefore, went so far as to boast about his weaknesses. He explained to the Corinthians that Christ's power rested on Paul in his weakness and made him strong enough to do what he wouldn't have been able to do on his own.

When we are aware of our weaknesses, of our need for Jesus, we yield ourselves more fully to God. We give Him room to move in and room to work. And He works not only in circumstances but also in our hearts. So, as Paul did, find delight in your weaknesses. Open them up to Him, and see God's great strength at work in you and through you.

Lord, You know my weaknesses, and You know the difficulties I'm dealing with. I ask You to show Your amazing strength through them.

2 Corinthians 12:7–10 NIV

He said to me, "My *grace* is sufficient for you, for my power is made *perfect* in weakness." Therefore I will boast all the more gladly about my weaknesses, so that Christ's *power* may rest on me. That is why, for Christ's sake, I delight in weaknesses, in insults, in hardships, in persecutions, in difficulties. For when I am weak, then I am *strong*.

THE GIFT OF FREEDOM

We often look for the fine print in life, watching for exceptions and exclusions. We mistrust that insurance policies will cover our needs, that warranties will still be in effect when the appliance breaks, or that we can really be free of our holy God's rightful punishment for past sins. Of course, it's good sense not to put all our faith in a manufacturer's guarantee. But we have no need to doubt the freedom from condemnation that Jesus Himself, God's perfect Lamb, grants us.

All of us have fallen short of God's standards for us (Romans 3:23). We deserve punishment, which in this case is death for our sins. But the good news is that Jesus took that punishment for us and we are forgiven! Paul wholeheartedly embraced the grace God gave us. Hear the confidence in this statement: "There is now no condemnation for those who are in Christ Jesus." No condemnation. Absolutely none.

You are forgiven and cleansed not because of what you do but because of what Christ did. You are forever free to live in God's grace and love, now and for eternity. Will you accept that freedom today?

Lord, help me rest in Your forgiveness and
live in the freedom of Your unfailing grace.

Romans 8:1 NIV

There is
now no
condemnation
for those who are
in Christ Jesus.

BE STILL . . .

The call to stillness in Psalm 46:10 seems especially difficult in our culture. But this challenge is nothing new.

Consider the prophet Elijah. He lived through countless dramatic events, even boldly rebuking the evil King Ahab and challenging the false prophets of Baal to a contest. After God won that dramatic showdown with fire falling from the sky, Queen Jezebel wanted Elijah killed. God protected Elijah when he ran for his life, but when he was alone with a price on his head, he felt hopeless. In response, God sent rock-breaking wind, an earthquake, a fire, and then "a still small voice" (1 Kings 19:12). The Lord did not minister to Elijah in the powerful acts of nature but through a soft whisper heard in the quiet.

God is spectacularly powerful. Yet He calls us to know Him not in the bombastic and loud noise but in the stillness. Big displays of power may be dazzling, but deep faith grows during our quiet communion with Him.

That God wants to draw near to us, that He wants to communicate with us, that we can hear His voice—aren't these the most astonishing miracles? Be still . . . and know that He is God.

*Lord, teach me to find quiet, to make
quiet, so that I can know You better.*

Psalm 46:10

"Be still,
and know
that I am
God."

CHANGER OF HEARTS

I'll pray for you." That's often our response when we hear about someone's hard times. And praying—inviting the all-powerful, all-loving God to work on a person's behalf—is definitely the right thing to do. But when we pray, why not ask God to touch hearts as well as circumstances?

We can learn from the way the apostle Paul prayed for the believers in Ephesus. He could have prayed for specific needs, but instead he prayed for their hearts.

Paul asked God to give them greater wisdom, knowledge, and understanding of Him. Paul wanted them to know the values, purpose, and work of God's kingdom. The apostle asked God to make hope very real to the Ephesians—to keep them focused on the future: eternal life. After all, God's power had raised Jesus from the dead, so it was certainly strong enough to tackle any situation the Ephesians were facing.

God invites us to pray about anything and everything we are concerned about. We are definitely free to mention the details. But as we pray for specific people or situations, let us also ask God to bless hearts with wisdom, knowledge, faith, and a mindfulness of His great power.

Lord, show me how to pray for others.
Grant them greater wisdom and a clearer
understanding of who You are.

Ephesians 1:17–19

[I pray] that the God of our Lord Jesus Christ, the Father of glory, may give to you the *spirit* of *wisdom* and revelation in the knowledge of Him, the eyes of your understanding being enlightened; that you may know what is the hope of His calling, what are the *riches* of the *glory* of His inheritance in the saints, and what is the exceeding greatness of His power toward us who believe.

THE LORD OUR ROCK

*L*ife's hurts raise hard questions. Why would God allow certain situations—and why is He slow to provide resolution and relief? Life is difficult, and the Bible doesn't suggest otherwise.

King David was facing difficult times when he penned Psalm 62. Yet David remembered that God was his rock, a secure foundation for life. When David was attacked, God was his fortress, a safe place to go for protection.

Now consider the last part of verse 2. Sounding entirely confident in his God, David proclaimed, "I will never be shaken." Nothing would rattle his faith! But the English Standard Version offers a glimpse of David's humanness: "I shall not be *greatly* shaken" (emphasis added). This translation may acknowledge the reality that events can shake—at least a little bit—the faith of even the most devoted follower. Yet the shaking isn't at the core of his convictions and doesn't last long. After all, the psalmist knows to turn to his Lord, who is his rock, his salvation, his fortress.

In this fallen world our faith may be shaken from time to time, but the Lord will never let us go.

Lord, You know when I'm feeling shaken.
Remind me that You are my rock and my
salvation, and that You will never let me go.

Psalm 62:2 NIV

Truly he
is my *rock* and
my *salvation*;
he is my
fortress,
I will never
be *shaken*.

JESUS SHOWED THE WAY

*J*esus calls us to serve one another, just as He served His disciples at the Last Supper by washing their dusty feet. Jesus calls us to love one another, just as He did when He let Himself be nailed to the cross so that we might be forgiven.

Yes, Jesus commands it, but He also lived it. He asks us to do nothing that He didn't do Himself.

In Philippians 2:9–11 we learn that God the Father, pleased with His Son, raised Jesus to the very highest level and gave Him a name that's "above every name" (NIV). So let's do the same. Let's put Jesus first when we make decisions. Let's not hold back in talking about Him or in living in a way that honors Him. Let's learn His will and change our lives to follow it, making our loving relationship with Him our top priority.

Consider the closing scene: one day God promises "every knee should bow, in heaven and on earth and under the earth, and every tongue acknowledge that Jesus Christ is Lord" (NIV). How amazing that time will be! And how wonderful it is that our praise of Jesus as Lord can start right now!

Lord, thank You that I can enjoy Your forgiveness, grace, and friendship both today and forever.

Philippians 2:9–11 NIV

Therefore God *exalted* him
to the highest place and gave
him the name that is above
every name, that at the name
of Jesus every knee should
bow, in *heaven* and on *earth*
and under the earth, and
every tongue acknowledge
that Jesus Christ is Lord, to
the *glory* of God the Father.

LIVING WORD

*D*id you know that more than forty authors wrote the Bible over a span of 1,500 to 1,800 years in three languages on three continents? On Scripture's pages readers can find history, biography, letters, parables, prophecies, sermons, and more. Despite this diversity, the Bible is a coherent work, unified in theme and purpose.

But this amazing piece of literature is not just a collection of fascinating documents. By the power of the Holy Spirit, it is living and active (Hebrews 4:12), as well as "profitable for doctrine, for reproof, for correction, for instruction in righteousness" (2 Timothy 3:16). No wonder God calls us to be *doers* of the Word, not just hearers (James 1:22). We meet as a community to study, share, and put God's Word into practice.

So where do you go to learn how to live and make a positive mark on the world? God's Word educates us, especially when we seek it corporately, so we "may be complete, thoroughly equipped for every good work" (2 Timothy 3:17). So equip yourself by studying God's Word, both individually and with others who seek Him too.

Lord God, help me become a dedicated student of Your Word, always letting You guide me and grow me through its pages.

2 Timothy 3:16–17

All Scripture is given
by *inspiration* of God,
and is profitable for
doctrine, for reproof, for
correction, for instruction
in *righteousness*, that the
man of God may be complete,
thoroughly equipped
for every *good* work.

JOYFUL GOD

*W*hat brings God joy and genuine pleasure? His people! He delights in those who have given their lives to Him and recognize that He is almighty God, deliverer, redeemer, and King. He delights in those who choose to serve Him with their lives. He is so pleased when His people obey Him and when they persevere in their faith. God loves when they talk to others about Jesus and why they serve Him. And their heartfelt praise of Him? It warms His heart.

Consider again the wonderful promises of Zephaniah 3:17. God is in your midst—in the midst of your schedule, your responsibilities, your home, your workplace, your church, your community, your nation. And this Mighty One will save: He will bring peace, redemption, guidance, and hope to any situation you—His child—find yourself in. And simply because you're His creation, He will rejoice over you with gladness and song. He will also come alongside to quiet you with His love when circumstances call for that. What a comforting promise.

The Lord your God is a God of joy. Know that He rejoices in you!

Almighty God, You give me countless reasons to rejoice. May I give You reasons to rejoice as well.

Zephaniah 3:17

The LORD your God
in your midst, the
Mighty One, will *save*;
He will *rejoice* over
you with gladness,
He will quiet you with
His love, He will rejoice
over you with *singing*.

SEIZE THE DAY

*E*ver since Horace penned *carpe diem* ("seize the day")—and probably long before that—philosophers, poets, and many others have urged us to make the most of the present. Here are a couple of examples:

> Finish each day and be done with it. . . . This day is all that is good and fair. It is too dear, with its hopes and invitations, to waste a moment on yesterdays.
>
> —RALPH WALDO EMERSON

> Don't look back on happiness, or dream of it in the future. You are only sure of today; do not let yourself be cheated out of it.
>
> —HENRY WARD BEECHER

These wise authors say basically the same thing, but the psalmist says it best. Why? Because the psalmist gives credit for the gift of today to the Lord, the One who made it and deserves the credit.

What will you do to seize today? Yes, we can learn from yesterday and from our mistakes and successes, but today deserves all of our attention. So choose to focus on the present, doing and saying things that reflect your gratitude to the Lord who made this day and gave it to you.

I am so grateful for this day, Lord. Teach me new ways to show it in my life.

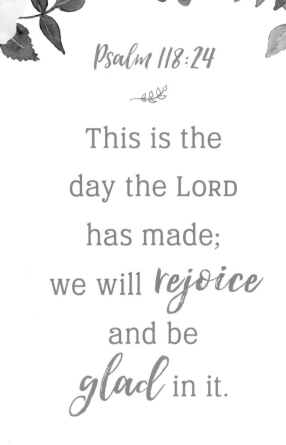

Psalm 118:24

This is the
day the LORD
has made;
we will *rejoice*
and be
glad in it.

HE WALKED IN OUR SHOES

*Y*ou've probably heard this popular saying more than once in your life: "You never truly know someone until you've walked a mile in his shoes." There is great value in being able to understand another person through common experience. That bond makes for a special connection of the heart.

It's possible for us to have that kind of heart connection with Jesus Himself because He left the throne of heaven and walked this earth for more than thirty years. The infinite God became finite. He cut teeth and skinned His knees. He learned to walk and talk and work in His father's carpentry shop. More importantly, the writer of Hebrews adds, Jesus "was in all points tempted as we are." In other words, He has walked in our shoes. He knows what we feel when we face temptation. He understands, and He will graciously help us stand strong.

To get this help, we must go "boldly to the throne of grace," and since Jesus knows firsthand the road we're walking, there's no reason for us to hesitate.

*Lord, thank You that when Jesus walked
in my shoes, He faced temptation and
won. Help me do as He did in all ways.*

Hebrews 4:15–16

We do not have a High Priest who cannot *sympathize* with our weaknesses, but was in all points tempted as we are, yet without sin. Let us therefore come *boldly* to the throne of *grace*, that we may obtain *mercy* and find grace to help in time of need.

HE HAS OVERCOME

Surely the day can't get any worse! You've probably had this thought on more days than you care to admit. The toast burns, the coffee spills, the kids don't cooperate. Then the car won't start, or the traffic won't move. Those are frustrations.

Then there are the tribulations. The doctor's diagnosis. The job loss. The unexpected death of a loved one. The estranged friendship. The church split. Jesus promised tribulations, and a sin-stained, fallen world promises frustrations.

Yet when we inevitably face frustrations and tribulations, God reminds us of some important truths. Our God is much greater than anything we face—He has overcome the world! He is still making us into what we will become, and He has a plan.

You can't unspill the coffee, open up the freeway, or change the doctor's diagnosis. You *can* choose to have faith that God is in control. He is not surprised or dismayed by the challenges you face. His plan for your life is still working itself out.

Yes, in this world you will have trouble, but the almighty God has overcome the world!

*God, thank You for this reminder that You are
bigger than any circumstance I encounter
and that nothing in this world will get in
the way of Your plans for my life.*

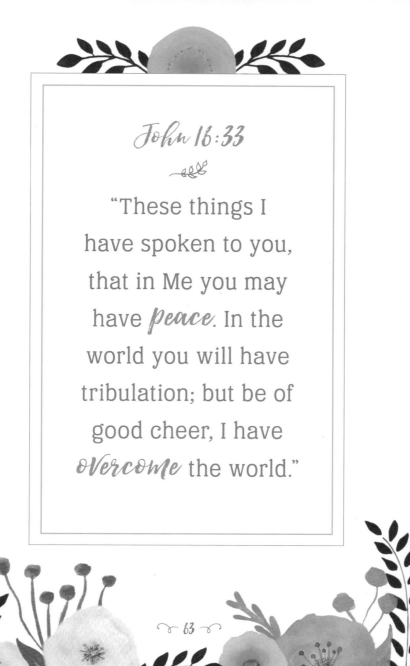

John 16:33

"These things I have spoken to you, that in Me you may have *peace*. In the world you will have tribulation; but be of good cheer, I have *overcome* the world."

FISH IN WATER

Surrounded by water, a fish is not aware of the weight of the water or conscious of the option of life on land. It doesn't know it's wet, because water is all it knows.

Similarly, living in a sinful world, we are not always aware of the weight of sin or even its presence and its wrongness. It's simply our environment. Until the Holy Spirit moves in our hearts, we aren't conscious of the fact that we could live a life free of sin, forgiven.

Once the Holy Spirit's freeing, transforming work in us is underway, we can become aware of sin—yet other people's sin is usually much more obvious to us than our own. That's why in Galatians 6:4–5 we are reminded to tend to our own sin.

We can't be the Holy Spirit for other people. We also can't compare ourselves to them. Instead, we are to keep our eyes on Jesus. Growing closer to Him will help us become more aware of our own sins so that, humbly, we can be cleansed of those sins. And then we can embrace the transforming power of Jesus in our lives.

Lord, continue to do Your convicting, cleansing, and transforming work in me, and help me keep my focus on Your holy Son.

Galatians 6:4–5 NCV

Each person should judge
his own actions and not
compare himself with others.
Then he can be *proud*
for what he himself has
done. Each person must be
responsible for himself.

LIKE GOLD

*S*ometimes it's a matter of perspective.

Think about a time you were disappointed or hurt. Look back on the relationship that ended or the move that uprooted you. By God's grace, the pain and heartache have faded through the years. Has your perspective on that experience changed as well?

You may have come to appreciate what you learned through that hard time. You may see how God used that crisis to move you to where He wanted you to be. Now you are genuinely thankful for the improvements He made. You might even be able to say that you would never trade in that bittersweet time for anything, because God was with you all the way.

Life's hard times aren't easy. Whichever word you choose—Job chose *tested*, but *pruned*, *refined*, *sanctified*, and *transformed* also work—you can be sure the process will be painful. But the blessings can be far greater than you might imagine. In the midst of his devastating losses, Job declared, "I shall come forth as gold."

Choose that perspective today. Your Redeemer God will not let the pain be for nothing. He will use it to make you strong in Him, reflecting His glory.

I praise You, God, that You use every experience in this fallen world to refine me for Your glory!

Job 23:10

But He knows the
way that I take;
when He has *tested*
me, I shall come
forth as *gold*.

THE REASON

Okay. You may not be Mother Teresa, but you can still have a significant impact on the people around you as you walk with God through life's good times and hard times. Think for a moment about the people God put along your path to encourage you in your faith. Though they might not be spiritual superstars, in God's view every one of those people has played an important role in His work.

So what about you? You could be that influence or encouragement to someone else. That's why God calls you to "be prepared to give an answer to everyone who asks you to give the reason for the hope that you have." Are you ready? You don't have to be a saint, theologian, or spiritual superstar. You're not the one who does the real heavy lifting—it's God. People can learn and be comforted by the faith you show through struggles. So when you open up to share with others about the hope that you have, silently give the situation over to God and let Him do His miraculous work. Rest and have confidence in the fact that your God is able to handle every situation and relationship.

*Lord, show me how to encourage others
in faith, and speak through me as I tell
them about the hope You give.*

1 Peter 3:15 NIV

In your hearts revere
Christ as Lord. Always
be prepared to give an
answer to everyone who
asks you to give the
reason for the *hope*
that you have. But do
this with *gentleness*
and *respect*.

JOYFUL STRENGTH

*D*espite having almost twenty-six miles behind them, marathon runners find a boost of energy when the finish line comes into view. The joy of achieving something longed for can give much-needed strength in a grueling challenge. Even more, joy in knowing the Lord is a sure source of strength for His people as they face the challenges, hurts, and disappointments of life.

Jesus offers us the ultimate example of finding strength in the joy of the Lord. Well aware that the cross awaited Him—as well as rejection, mockery, betrayal, denial, and scourging—Jesus was resolved to go to Jerusalem. Luke reported that "He steadfastly set His face to go to Jerusalem" (Luke 9:51). Why was Jesus able to keep moving forward? The author of Hebrews explained that it was because of "the joy that was set before Him [that Jesus] endured the cross" (12:2).

You are undoubtedly bearing a cross of your own. After all, Jesus promised that His people would know trials and tribulations in this world (John 16:33). Yet in communion with God, you can know joy despite life's circumstances.

When I look to You instead of at my situation, I find reasons for joy. Thank You for sustaining me.

Nehemiah 8:10

The *joy*

of the

LORD is your

strength.

COMFORT IN THE NIGHT

A restless night, a bout of insomnia, unsettling dreams— for various reasons, we don't always experience the simple gift of renewing sleep. But sometimes the reasons are actually a matter of faith.

Are you worried about a situation? Are you stewing over a decision you need to make? Are you aching over a loss? If things like these are keeping you awake, consider inviting the Lord into your sleeping hours.

When you lie in bed awake, pray. Pray constantly, thankfully, about everything—and watch for evidence of His presence and His work in your life. Lay at His feet your concerns or looming decisions. Confess your worries, especially if you find it hard to trust Him. That simple step of confession may in itself bring peace.

If the struggle continues, choose a verse of Scripture to meditate on, like today's verse. You could also ask God to remind you of examples of His great faithfulness, and continue to lay before Him any and every concern that is weighing you down and keeping you awake. Like David in Psalm 3, celebrate the Lord's sustaining power, even in your worries, and you will see a lighter tomorrow.

Father, when I can't sleep, help me take my worries to You so I can be filled with Your peace.

Psalm 3:5–6

I lay down and slept;
I awoke, for the Lord
sustained me. I will
not be afraid of ten
thousands of people
who have set themselves
against me all around.

KEEP CHOOSING GOD

Think for a moment about how many choices you make in a day. Some are pretty minor (what to have for breakfast), and other choices may be rather significant (whether to accept that job offer). Some decisions are one-time, once-and-for-all: if you decide to be a parent and become one, for instance, you're always a parent. Other decisions need to be made again and again.

The decision to serve the Lord definitely falls into that second category. This choice comes up several times a day as we find ourselves facing the same question God asked the people of Israel through Joshua: Whom will you serve?

When it comes to everyday decisions like whether to be gracious to someone who has irritated you, letting a stressed mom go before you in the grocery line, or choosing whether to gossip, whom will you serve?

With the bigger issues like adultery, lying, or murder, for instance, the choice seems more obvious. But all those *little issues* raise the same question: Whom will you serve? Will you serve God by doing the loving, kind, selfless, and difficult thing? Or will you serve yourself? The choice is yours.

God, help me serve You in the simple moments of an ordinary day as well as in the big issues of life.

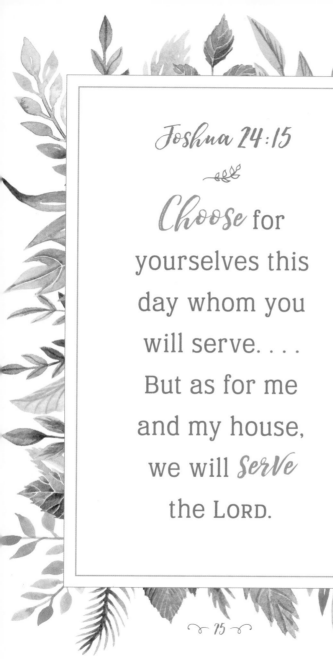

Joshua 24:15

Choose for
yourselves this
day whom you
will serve. . . .
But as for me
and my house,
we will *serve*
the Lord.

THE GIFT OF GRACE

*I*t doesn't make sense. There's got to be a catch.

Nope. It's clear in Ephesians: your salvation is a gift. You can't negotiate a peace treaty with the holy God. You can't earn a ticket to heaven by behaving better than your neighbor. God doesn't grade on a curve. You simply have to believe.

And these are the basics to believe in: God is holy. We are sinners. Jesus died on the cross to bridge this gap between God and us. His death paid the price for our sin, and His resurrection proved that He is the Son of God. And because of Him, we can live in relationship with our heavenly Father, now and forever.

Those are the basics of the Christian faith. Do you believe? And if so, do you realize that even your belief in the gospel truth is a gift? God even helps you believe!

This gift of the gospel doesn't make sense to those who know there's no such thing as a free lunch. But there truly is no catch. Simply humble yourself to receive God's gifts of forgiveness, faith, and salvation. Then say thank You by living a life characterized by trust, love, and obedience.

Lord, You call me to stop striving, to
humble myself, and to simply receive
Your love. What amazing grace!

Ephesians 2:8–9

By grace you have been *saved* through *faith*, and that not of yourselves; it is the *gift* of God, not of works, lest anyone should boast.

GOD'S RIGHT HAND

*I*t makes sense: we would not need to be told to "fear not" if there were nothing to fear. There must be things in this world, in this life, to which fear is a logical and even natural response.

Notice that when God says, "Fear not," He doesn't stop with just those two words. He knows you can't flip a switch and simply turn off your fear. So He immediately gives the watertight reason not to fear: "for I am with you."

What does that mean? It means that God Himself will provide His people with strength, He will help His people, and He will hold on to His people with His righteous right hand. That right hand represents God's power and His authority over sin and over His people. He holds you in a place of complete security—He is not some distant being; neither is He too busy to attend to you. He declares that He is *your* God.

So when you're feeling fearful, turn to your God, for He is already with you—strengthening, helping, and upholding you.

> *God, thank You that I am never alone*
> *because You are with me and I do not*
> *need to fear when I call out for You.*

Isaiah 41:10

"Fear not, for I am with you; be not dismayed, for I am your God. I will *strengthen* you, yes, I will help you, I will uphold you with My *righteous* right hand."

A HOLY FOCUS

*I*n case you haven't noticed, we live in a very noisy world. Stop reading for a moment and consider all the sounds around you. Do you hear cars, horns, airplanes, a ringing phone, conversation, the TV, music, or all of the above? And then there is the more personal noise we can add to our lives with our own phones and computers.

That noise isn't all innocent. Some of it promotes values that aren't in line with God's standards, words that dishonor Him and disrespect other people, statements that glorify sin and decadence, or arguments for issues that are unbiblical. All of this makes obedience to Philippians 4:8 very difficult. It isn't easy to crowd out the noise.

So it makes total sense that God calls on us, His people, to replace the noise by thinking about whatever is true, noble, right, pure, lovely, admirable, excellent, and praiseworthy. Starting each day by reading His Word will fill our minds with what is worth thinking about, as will listening to music that glorifies Him and spending time talking with fellow believers whose words reflect their relationship with God. Today, ask the Holy Spirit to keep you always looking to Jesus, the most excellent and praiseworthy One.

In this noisy world, Lord, help me listen
for and hear Your still, small voice.

Philippians 4:8 NIV

Finally, brothers and sisters, whatever is true, whatever is *noble*, whatever is right, whatever is *pure*, whatever is lovely, whatever is admirable—if anything is *excellent* or praiseworthy— think about such things.

READY FOR BATTLE

King David was not only a shepherd but also a warrior. He knew the battlefield—its demands, the strategies for success, the roles that courage and faith play, and which weapons were necessary for victory and survival. No wonder he talks about God and life in military terms in many of his psalms.

This battle imagery continues in the New Testament— the battle between God and Satan is still very real. Paul wrote, "We do not wrestle against flesh and blood, but against principalities, against powers, against the rulers of the darkness of this age" (Ephesians 6:12).

So David's ancient words about God as his strength, his shield, and his refuge are as relevant today as they were on the Israelite battlefield centuries ago. We still need Him to be the source of our strength, our shield of protection from the powers of darkness, and our refuge from "principalities" that want our destruction. We would also do well to follow David's example of rejoicing in the Lord and praising Him with song, knowing that He has already won the battle!

My enemies aren't visible, Lord, but I know
the battle rages. Please be my shield as
I fight to stand strong in my faith.

Psalm 28:7–8

The LORD is my *strength*
and my *shield*; my heart
trusted in Him, and I
am helped; therefore my
heart greatly rejoices, and
with my song I will *praise*
Him. The LORD is their
strength, and He is the saving
refuge of His anointed.

GOD'S NEW GENERATION

*W*hen you think of the younger generation, do you picture an entitled, selfish, fussy, or aimless group of coddled individuals? That may be a popular image, but many of our young people are strong, responsible, and fighting to defy such low expectations. They are our future. Why would we write them off?

Instead, ask yourself what you could be doing to encourage young people. How can you encourage new believers—those young in their faith—to live out God's commandments, to grow in their knowledge of Jesus, and to be His light in the world? Paul wrote that youth is not to be despised, that God uses both young and old for His kingdom work. Ask the Lord to help your attitudes and actions reflect that truth.

How are you being an example? If you're not sure you're doing much of anything right now, ask Jesus to show you a relationship to invest in, a sin or character trait to work on changing, or even a specific ministry to get involved in. He will guide you in your efforts.

Thank You for the younger generation. Help me be an example to them and all believers in word, in conduct, in love, and for Your glory.

1 Timothy 4:12

Let no one despise
your youth, but be an
example to the
believers in word, in
conduct, in love, in spirit,
in *faith*, in purity.

HOPE FOR TROUBLED HEARTS

*J*esus had washed His disciples' feet. *Puzzling. Humiliating!* Jesus had predicted His betrayal and, as He dipped bread with Judas Iscariot, identified the betrayer. *Shocking! Infuriating!* Now Jesus had just told His disciples that He would not be with them much longer. *What? Why?*

Good-hearted and impulsive as always, Peter proclaimed that he wanted to follow Jesus wherever He was going. Peter even vowed to lay down his life for his Lord. Jesus simply responded with the statement that Peter would deny even knowing Him before the rooster crowed. The mood at the Last Supper grew even more somber.

Jesus knew that His disciples would soon need hope. He knows that you need hope too, the kind of hope that makes the earth's darkness less oppressive. That's why He told them, "I go to prepare a place for you," a hope-filled promise that can help you put one foot in front of the other when the darkness is almost tangible.

What is troubling your heart right now? What does it mean that Jesus has gone before you to prepare a place for you with Him in eternity? Have hope; no matter how dark it seems, Jesus has secured your future.

Jesus, what comfort it is to know that
You understand feeling troubled. Thank
You for all You did to give me hope.

John 14:1–3

"Let not your heart be troubled;
you believe in God, believe
also in Me. In My Father's
house are many mansions; if
it were not so, I would have
told you. I go to *prepare* a
place for you. And if I go
and prepare a place for you,
I will come again and *receive*
you to Myself; that where I
am, there you may be also."

OUR SUN AND SHIELD

*I*t's no cosmic coincidence: the Earth is the perfect distance from the sun for sustaining life. This ideal distance means Earth has water and the right temperatures to support plants and animals.

But even without knowing this, the psalmist was well aware of some key facts when he wrote, "The LORD God is a sun." The psalmist recognized that God is the source of life, the One who enables us to experience abundant life here on Earth and eternal life with Him. Just as sunlight means health, growth, and light, God's presence means the same thing in the physical and spiritual lives of His people.

The psalmist also recognized God as a shield of protection, as well as the giver of favor and honor. His blessings will, however, vary with His people's obedience: "No good thing does he withhold from those who walk uprightly."

So to show the Lord your love, walk in obedience to His ways. After all, He is the perfectly distanced sun who gives you life.

God, thank You that Jesus came the perfect distance—from heaven to earth—to help me know Your love and Your forgiveness.

Psalm 84:11 ESV

For the LORD God is
a *sun* and *shield*;
the LORD bestows
favor and *honor*.
No good thing
does he withhold
from those who
walk uprightly.

LOOK TO JESUS

everal things can keep us from running a good race in this life. We may be lugging around heavy burdens of self-made laws, regret, hurt, and worry. We can also be tripped up by sin, and we can choose to believe the lie that we can't run another step. Consider the better option: look to Jesus!

Trying to find security in people's approval is like heaping an unnecessary burden upon ourselves. The more we look to others, the more dissatisfied we'll be with ourselves. Why? Because people are imperfect, and they are changeable. God, on the other hand, will never change, waver, or abandon us, and He always has our best interests in mind.

So if you're feeling the pressure of pleasing others and find yourself always falling short, look away from yourself and toward your Father. He is the key to knowing security, joy, and hope in this life. Fixing your eyes on Jesus can also help you keep your priorities straight and simplify your day because you know where you're going, why you're going, and with whom you're going. Such simplicity and security are blessings indeed.

Lord, please guide me back to You when I look elsewhere for purpose and significance.

Hebrews 12:1–2

Since we are surrounded
by so great a cloud of
witnesses, let us lay aside
every weight, and the sin which
so easily ensnares us, and
let us run with *endurance*
the race that is set before us,
looking unto Jesus, the author
and *finisher* of our *faith*.

THE END OF PAIN

*J*esus didn't try to sugarcoat the truth. He told us that we will encounter suffering during our years on this planet. Loss and betrayal will be part of our lives just as they were for Jesus Himself. We will be lonely and misunderstood just as He was. We may be falsely accused, unfairly condemned, and treated poorly, and Jesus knows about that firsthand too. The path we walk on this earth is watered with our tears.

God knows those tears. He is with us always, whatever pain comes our way and whatever darkness blinds us to His presence. He is the God of all compassion and comfort. He knows that the fires of life can ravage His people, and He brings beauty out of ashes.

More wonderful than the truth that God knows and redeems our pain is the fact that one day He "will wipe away every tear." What a picture of His tender love! And one day there will be no more tears, "no more death, nor sorrow, nor crying . . . [and] no more pain." What a picture of a redeemed world!

Come quickly, Lord!

Thank You for redeeming our suffering, Lord.
Even as I praise You, I look forward to the day of
Your total victory over sin, death, and sorrow.

Revelation 21:4

"God will wipe away
every *tear* from their eyes;
there shall be no more
death, nor *sorrow*,
nor *crying*. There shall be
no more pain, for the former
things have passed away."

RENEWED TRUST

*I*t's easy to listen to words but not actually hear them, just as we can look at people but not really see them. We can become blind to beauty we see all the time and numb to truths we hear often. In light of this, read Proverbs 3:5–6 again, as if it's the first time you've read it.

Next, as an exercise, put these verses in your own words. It might go something like this: "In everything you think about or worry about, trust in God. He is able to direct any situation, even when you don't understand what's going on. Your worries and challenges can be used for your growth and good. Acknowledge Him by asking for His guidance in every situation, and feel His strength and guidance as you carry on down your path, no matter how steep it may be."

In what areas of your life are you struggling to trust Jesus? In what current situation do you need to lean more heavily on Him through trust? Ask the Lord to reignite your passion for Him, to help you release any self-reliant attitudes, and to embrace the growth opportunities in your path.

In everything, simply trust in the Lord.

*Thank You, Holy Spirit, for helping me
hear familiar truths with new ears.*

Proverbs 3:5–6

Trust in the Lord with
all your *heart*, and
lean not on your own
understanding; in all your
ways *acknowledge* Him, and
He shall direct your paths.

COUNT IT ALL JOY

*C*ount it *all* joy? That sounds like an impossible assignment, doesn't it? Think about the current "various trials" in your life. What is making it tough for you to find joy? Pain? Fear? The unknown? Something else?

Yes, to "count it all joy" is a tough assignment. It was certainly so for the early believers who were persecuted for their faith. They knew what it was to suffer because they loved Jesus. But James clearly reminded them—and he reminds us—that God is aware of those trials and is present in them. God uses trials to strengthen us and grow greater patience and resilience within us (vv. 3–4).

How does God help us find "all joy"? One way is through His promises. We know from His Word that He can and does redeem the most difficult life experiences. We also know the ultimate security: we will spend eternity with Him. That promise can help us remember that there's more to life than what this world has for us.

So choose to rejoice not *for* life's trials but *despite* them. After all, God is with you on the journey, He will not let you go, and He promises you eternal life.

Lord God, thank You for reminding me
that earthly pain and joy are transitory,
but Your promises are forever.

James 1:2-3

My brethren, count it
all *joy* when you fall
into various trials,
knowing that the
testing of your *faith*
produces *patience*.

A BOLD SPIRIT

*D*o you ever feel nervous about offending people when talking about your faith? In some circles, speaking openly about Christianity can provoke anger or even get you labeled as a fanatic or a bigot. Believers in other parts of the world actually face violence or death for their faith in Jesus. That's why all Christians need to be encouraged to be bold about the gospel. As Paul put it, "God has not given us a spirit of fear."

Fear is a tool the Enemy uses to discourage God's people from taking a stand for Him. So when fear rises, reject the Enemy's lies in the powerful name of Jesus and act in love—despite the fear.

Instead of fear, God has blessed us with power, love, and a sound mind. The Spirit will give us the strength to speak boldly and the sensitivity to speak at the right times. When God calls us to speak, He empowers us with words to do it well. The Spirit will help us love the ones we share with and to think clearly as we speak to them. He is in our corner, so we can speak with confidence.

You, Lord, are stronger than he who is in the world. Guide me as I share Your truth without fear, and help me love all those You have put in my life.

2 Timothy 1:7

God has not

given us a

spirit of fear,

but of *power* and

of *love* and of a

sound mind.

HEAVENLY RICHES

*W*isdom, power, and wealth—God warns us against finding glory in these. Graduate and honorary degrees reflect a certain amount of learning but not necessarily wisdom. Strength can be indicated by pounds bench-pressed and miles run, but injury and aging take their toll. Riches can be measured by assets, but fire and international economics can steal these away. Still, we hunger for the honor that comes with being thought wise, mighty, or rich.

Consider, however, that God calls us to glory in the fact that we know Him—the God of the universe! Knowing Him means seeing when He is "exercising lovingkindness, judgment, and righteousness in the earth." You find hope and peace in His coming justice, you see His righteousness in His commands, and you look forward to His return to earth.

What a privilege to know the almighty God! As you read God's Word, worship the Lord, and pray to Him. Take joy in the honor it is to communicate with Him.

You know, Father, how attractive worldly
accomplishments can be. Steer me toward
You and godly wealth that lasts for eternity.

Jeremiah 9:23–24

"Let not the wise man glory in his *wisdom*, let not the mighty man *glory* in his might, nor let the rich man glory in his riches; but let him who glories glory in this, that he *understands* and knows Me, that I am the LORD, exercising lovingkindness, judgment, and righteousness in the earth."

HAPPILY EVER AFTER

$\mathcal{S}$ome of us tend to grab onto Romans 8:28 as a kind of good luck charm. It sounds like a glorious guarantee of a happily-ever-after life for those who call Jesus their Lord and Savior.

But is this verse truly a happily-ever-after promise? Look again at the end of Romans 8:28: God works for the good of those (1) who love Him and (2) whom He has called according to His purpose for them. Verse 29 explains that purpose: God wants His people to become more like Jesus.

Jesus is patient and kind. Jesus is not envious or proud, and He is not easily angered. He doesn't have a record of all the wrongs we've done. He does not delight in any evil in the world; instead, He honors truth. He protects, trusts, hopes, and perseveres (1 Corinthians 13:4–7). God uses every event, relationship, challenge, and hurt that we experience to make us more like Jesus. Our experiences become the tools God uses to teach us to let go of pride and anger, and to instead protect, trust, hope, and persevere—just like Jesus. No one can improve on that happily ever after.

God, thank You for caring more about my Christlikeness than my happiness. Transform me so I can glorify You in this life.

Romans 8:28–29 NIV

We know that in all things God *works* for the good of those who love him, who have been called according to his *purpose*. For those God foreknew he also predestined to be *conformed* to the image of his Son, that he might be the firstborn among many brothers and sisters.

NEVER-ENDING GRACE

*D*on't we find it easier to see other people's sin than our own? We also do a fine job of comparing our sins with the sins of others—and declaring theirs are much worse. But every sin ever committed—ours included—sent Jesus to the cross.

The sins of King David, a man after God's own heart and the author of Psalm 51, also sent Jesus to the cross. And among those sins were adultery, deception, framing a loyal military leader, murder, cover-up, and pride. He certainly put God's grace to the test!

But David isn't the only one. We all need grace on a daily basis. We disobey, break His law, and act irresponsibly—and we do it over and over again. It almost makes us think that we'll push God to His limit—that one day the straw will break the camel's back, and He will refuse to forgive us. But that's the thing about grace: it has no end. No matter how bad we think we've messed up this time, when we return to Him and ask for His forgiveness, God's grace is enough to put us back together again. And that is very good news!

Lord, when I get frustrated with myself, it is good to know that You will never run out of grace for me.

Psalm 51:1–2

Have mercy upon me,
O God, according to Your
lovingkindness; according
to the multitude of Your
tender mercies, blot out
my *transgressions*.
Wash me thoroughly
from my iniquity, and
cleanse me from my sin.

NEW CREATURES

*P*icture a butterfly. What was once a caterpillar has become a new creation. The transformation was not immediate; the process took time. And if the caterpillar could speak, it might have asked what was happening. Why did it have to go through the dark season of isolation when nothing of value seemed to be happening? But in the end, the new creation was glorious. No longer confined to crawling on the ground, the butterfly knew the freedom of flight.

Our redemption—that newness in Christ—changes us just as that caterpillar was changed. Because of Him, our old mistakes and priorities are wiped away. What was important to us then just isn't as important after we come to know the risen Christ. We have a new view of the world because we are new creatures, no longer crawling in sin but flying with Christ.

We still need to stand strong against sin, but we are freed from its control. Redeemed believers are open to God's ongoing transformational work in their lives so that, like that butterfly, they can enjoy the freedom that comes with the forgiveness, love, and grace God continuously pours out on His people.

God, thank You for the transforming work
You have begun and continue to do in my life.
Help me reflect Your goodness and love.

2 Corinthians 5:17

If anyone is in Christ,
he is a new *creation*;
old things have passed
away; *behold*, all things
have become new.

SEASONED WITH GRACE

God spoke the universe into existence. Satan spoke words of deceit to Eve that led to the entry of sin into the world. Jesus spoke life-changing words of forgiveness and healing. Words are powerful for good and for bad; they can build people up or tear them down.

Think about words you remember from your childhood, a favorite professor, a longtime friend, or Scripture. Perhaps the negatives have stuck with you more than the positives. In the same way, words we have spoken have either built people up or torn them down. Those are really the only two options.

In Colossians 4:6 God calls us to the positive option: He instructs us to season our speech with grace just as we season our food with salt. Salt enhances the taste of food and is a good preservative. Similarly, the grace of our words should enhance our message and preserve rather than destroy the hearts of those to whom we speak.

Consider carefully the impact your words have on the people you talk to. Ask the Holy Spirit to bless your self-control and give you the ability to think before you speak so your speech will always be "with grace."

Lord, transform me, and teach me to speak only words that You want me to speak.

Colossians 4:6 NASB

Let your speech
always be with *grace*,
as though seasoned
with salt, so that you will
know how you should
respond to each person.

CAUSE AND EFFECT

*G*IGO: garbage in; garbage out. This basic principle in computer programming asserts that the quality of the output is directly dependent on the quality of the input. If the program is flawed, the information it produces will be flawed. It's the simple law of cause and effect.

A word of caution: even a little bit of garbage can have a huge impact. Do you remember when one "little goof" cost NASA a $125 million Mars probe? The mistake was simple enough: some engineers were using inches and feet; others were using metric measurements. Oops! GIGO!

This principle applies to us too. When we put garbage into our hearts and minds, we shouldn't be surprised when garbage comes out. But let's focus on the positive corollary here: if what we put into our hearts and minds is godly and pure, what comes out of us—our words, actions, attitudes, and thoughts—will be much more pleasing to God.

Garbage in—allowing inappropriate TV, music, or media to influence our lives—means soon the garbage will be coming out! So pray what David wisely prayed: "Let the words of my mouth and the meditation of my heart be acceptable in Your sight."

God, please help me choose to fill my mind and heart with only good things.

Psalm 19:14

Let the words of
my mouth and the
meditation of my
heart be acceptable
in Your sight, O
Lord, my *strength*
and my Redeemer.

THE LORD PROVIDES

*N*eeds versus wants. In our culture the line between the two has been blurred. Yet it's important to understand the difference, especially in light of today's verse. Jesus felt it worthwhile to remind us that the Lord knows exactly what we, His children, need. Aware of our tendency to worry about what we will eat and what we will wear, Jesus declared, "Your heavenly Father knows that you need all these things" (Matthew 6:32). We can trust Him to meet those needs. The food may not be gourmet; the clothes may not be designer. But any expectations of filet mignon and Gucci labels reflect our desires rather than our needs.

The apostle Paul knew what it was like to be in need. So when the faithful members of the church at Philippi sent Paul a sacrificial gift in support of his ministry, he thanked them and the Lord. Then Paul encouraged those brothers and sisters with the truth of Philippians 4:19.

Gracious and generous, our Father always provides for His children out of His infinite resources. He faithfully meets our needs, and He often does so in ways far greater than we could have imagined.

God, thank You for reminding me that You will meet all my needs in this life and for eternity.

Philippians 4:19 NLT

This same
God who takes
care of me will
supply all your needs
from his *glorious* riches,
which have been given
to us in Christ Jesus.

OUR INFINITE GOD

*T*he heavens declare the glory of God" (Psalm 19:1)! They speak of His majesty, His power, His design, and even His love.

The order of the heavens, the complexity of a DNA molecule, the miracle of birth, the beauty of color and music and light—everywhere we turn we see our Creator's fingerprints in this world. Those fingerprints speak not only of His existence but also of His ongoing involvement in His creation and, more importantly, of His love not just for mankind in general but His love for you in particular.

Take some time this week to look—really look—at God's creation. If you can, go somewhere far from city lights and take in the night sky. Marvel at those billions of perfect stars that were created by the same hand that formed you and made you who you are.

Yes, our infinite God holds the planets in their orbits, but He also calls you by name and numbers the hairs on your head (Isaiah 43:1; Matthew 10:30). What amazing love! Take some time today to get outdoors, be alone with your Father, and listen for what He has to say just to you.

Father, thank You for this moment today to pause and consider Your amazing creation.

Isaiah 40:12–13

Who has measured the waters
in the hollow of His hand,
measured *heaven* with a
span and calculated the dust
of the *earth* in a measure?
Weighed the mountains
in scales and the hills in a
balance? Who has directed the
Spirit of the LORD, or as His
counselor has taught Him?

SEEK HIM FIRST

*S*eek first the kingdom of God." This is simple to understand, but not always easy to live, right?

The instruction to seek God's kingdom comes near the end of Jesus' Sermon on the Mount, which touched on wealth, worries, and trust. Knowing human nature, Jesus cautioned His audience against focusing on worldly acquisitions, loving money, and worrying about basic life necessities, so He reminded His listeners that God will take care of them just as He takes care of the birds each day. As the culminating point of His sermon, Jesus declared that God knows His people's needs and will provide for them. On the heels of that truth came the command to "seek first the kingdom of God and His righteousness" with the promise that "all these things shall be added to you."

Today, choose to move your focus from "all these things" to "the kingdom of God." Of course, you have to take care of daily business, but do it with the belief in your heart that your daily needs will be provided for. And as you do the work of His kingdom, you will see God's provision in your life time and again.

Lord, please help me work for Your
kingdom every moment, trusting that
You have all my needs in hand.

Matthew 6:33

"Seek first the kingdom of God and His *righteousness*, and all these things shall be added to you."

THE HUNT FOR JOY

*H*ow many red lights did you hit on the way home today? Did other lines at the grocery store or gas station move more quickly than yours? Did other people's kids behave better at the park than yours?

It's human nature to notice the small irritations, but this makes it difficult to find joy in daily life. It instead keeps us focused on ourselves and on how unfair life can be sometimes.

But we don't have to live like that. We can learn to obey the command of Philippians 4:4: to rejoice—always! Note that Paul didn't say to rejoice about our *circumstances*. Instead, we are to rejoice in the Lord—in His sovereign power, His unwavering goodness, and His unfailing love. When, despite all that is going on in life, we find in Him reasons to rejoice—and there are plenty—we will know His blessings of hope and peace.

So train yourself to look for evidence of God's presence in your life. Hunt for it like treasure, and share your findings. These seeds of joy will grow into even more joy!

Lord, reveal to me the many reasons
to praise You and rejoice in You, and
help me look for You always.

Philippians 4:4

Rejoice in the Lord *always*. Again I will say, *rejoice*!

PARTNER WITH GOD

*T*his principle worked in college, especially during exams: "Study like you don't pray—and pray like you don't study." The same idea is at work in today's psalm. We are to give our best effort to the task God has given us, all the while praying faithfully, asking God for His guidance, strength, and blessing in our work. When we try to do anything in our own power, for our own glory, our efforts will either fail or fall far short of what could have been with God's blessing.

God invites us into partnership with Him. Our part is to work to the best of our abilities to do God's will. We trust that He will do His part: He will show us what to do, enable us to do it, and bless our work. But if we try to do it alone, if we're building a house that God hasn't called us to build, we "labor in vain."

What task, if any, are you working on without the Lord's involvement or a sense of His presence with you? Ask God what He wants you to do. Listen for His answer. Then trust Him as you obey Him.

Lord, thank You for allowing me to partner
with You in Your work. Help me to do
the work You've called me to do.

Psalm 127:1

Unless the LORD builds
the house, they *labor*
in vain who build it;
unless the LORD *guards*
the city, the watchman
stays awake in vain.

TAKING UP THE CROSS

*T*hink about your initial response to Jesus' invitation to take up your cross and follow Him. Doesn't sound very pleasant, does it? Especially in Jesus' day, the cross meant agony and death. Today it can mean struggle, heartache, and humiliation, and in some cases, it can still mean agony and death. Taking up our own cross can seem less than appealing, yet accepting the invitation is inherent in our decision to follow Jesus.

We cannot live for ourselves, according to our own desires and dreams, and follow Jesus at the same time. Of course, Jesus' plans for us may match our desires and dreams, but His plans may also include the painful exercise of dying to our own ideas about the course of our lives.

So how do you take up your cross? By doing what Jesus did. That means setting our resolve and realigning our will with His at every step, even if the process seems as cumbersome as dragging a heavy cross up a hill. Jesus obeyed despite how much it hurt, and God raised Him up in glory. Let's follow His example.

Lord, when I'm struggling to take up my cross,
help me keep my eyes on You, knowing that
You will bless me when I do Your will.

Mark 8:34–36

"Whoever desires to come after Me, let him deny himself, and take up his *cross*, and follow Me. For whoever *desires* to save his life will lose it, but whoever loses his life for My sake and the gospel's will *save* it. For what will it profit a man if he gains the whole world, and *loses* his own soul?"

THE WORD IS THE WAY

*D*on't you love GPS and mapping apps? They prevent wrong turns, backtracking, aimless wandering, and even spousal arguments. With clear directions at our fingertips, we can sit back and enjoy the ride.

God's Word serves as a kind of GPS for His people. Knowing His Word and obeying it can keep us on the path God wants us to walk. We need only to hide its truth in our heart so we can better discern what goes on around us. The world offers its temptations and distractions, and the Enemy is subtle and persuasive in his deceitful schemes. Staying on God's narrow path becomes more and more difficult, but that is nothing new.

Consider God's message to Joshua: know Scripture, meditate on the Lord's truth, be careful to obey His commands, and know His blessings. That message is for us too. And now, on this side of the cross, we have not only God's Word but also the example of Christ and the indwelling Holy Spirit to provide guidance and strength for the journey of life. God has given His people all we need to walk in His way for all time.

Lord, thank You for Your provision.
Help me make choices that will keep
me on the path You have for me.

Joshua 1:8 NASB

"This book of the law shall not depart from your mouth, but you shall *meditate* on it day and night, so that you may be *careful* to do according to all that is written in it; for then you will make your way *prosperous*, and then you will have success."

PRESS ON

*D*o you know where you're going on this journey of life? The apostle Paul did. He had been traveling to Damascus to persecute Christians there, but after meeting the risen Lord on the road to the city, he received a new and clearly defined mission.

Like many other Jews, Paul had failed to recognize the Messiah while He was teaching in Jerusalem, but now Paul knew better. God had sent His only Son as a sacrifice for the sin of every one of us—past, present, and future. That was news worth sharing, and Paul accepted the assignment wholeheartedly.

We could let ourselves be bogged down by our past sin, but the truth is that we can do nothing to change what has already been done. We need to move on just as Paul did, accepting God's forgiveness and serving Christ with all that we are.

The apostle Paul's overriding priority was to serve the Lord. Likewise, let's focus on the goal of serving Jesus in whatever capacity He calls us. We have a Savior worth serving with all our heart, soul, mind, and strength!

God, thank You for calling me to know Jesus as my Savior. Help me press on toward the goals You've put in my life.

Philippians 3:12–14

Not that I have already attained, or am already *perfected*; but I press on, that I may lay hold of that for which Christ Jesus has also laid hold of me. Brethren, I do not *count* myself to have apprehended; but one thing I do, forgetting those things which are behind and reaching *forward* to those things which are ahead, I press toward the goal for the *prize* of the upward call of God in Christ Jesus.

THE SPIRIT SPEAKS FOR US

*T*hose who have experienced grief know that a person's presence is more significant than their words. Being near someone who is going through hard times speaks eloquently of love and concern; the hurting person doesn't need clichés or explanations or, at times, even Scripture verses.

When we are hurting, we know that no one's words can make the situation better or the heart less heavy. In fact, we don't always have words of our own to cry out to the Lord. The hurt is just too deep.

That's when we can ask the Spirit to help us. We grieve, and we ask Him to pray on our behalf. While we wait in our weakness, He "makes intercession for us." It may take time before we feel we can pray again. And that's okay. All we have to do is admit our own power is not enough to get us through. When we open our hearts to Him, God steps in and begins to heal us.

The Spirit prays for us even as He comforts us. And all the while, God does His work of healing and sowing seeds of hope.

Holy Spirit, when pain overwhelms me or I
need to make a tough decision, You know
how to pray—and You do pray. Thank You.

Romans 8:26

The Spirit also *helps* in our weaknesses. For we do not know what we should *pray* for as we ought, but the Spirit Himself makes *intercession* for us with groanings which cannot be uttered.

THE SOURCE OF STRENGTH

*M*aybe it's the solid job. Maybe it's the savings accounts, carefully diversified and monitored. Maybe it's the extended family, always there for you. Maybe it's your good health. We can get strength from a variety of sources, but only One will be fully reliable.

Moses knew that truth: God is the only reliable source of strength. Moses had personally encountered God, first in the burning bush (Exodus 3) and later on Mount Sinai when God delivered the Ten Commandments (Exodus 20). Moses had also personally experienced God's faithfulness during the forty-year exodus—the children of Israel never missed a meal thanks to the Lord's provision (Exodus 16). So, with total confidence in his Lord, Moses told Joshua and all of Israel to trust not in their own strength but in the strength of their unfailing God.

As you walk with the Lord through your wildernesses, as you recognize your heavenly Father's faithful provision, you will know with certainty that God will never "forsake you." So do not be afraid of your current circumstances; instead, rely on God—and Him alone—for your strength.

Lord, show me how to trust in Your strength alone,
and give me the courage I need to rely on You.

Deuteronomy 31:6 NIV

Be strong and courageous. Do not be afraid or terrified because of them, for the Lord your God goes with you; he will never leave you nor forsake you.

HEALTHY HUMILITY

*T*he word *humility* can bring to mind some negative associations, like the unhealthy choice to be a doormat for others or never speaking up for yourself. But none of that is biblical, godly, or Christlike humility. Being humble before God is acknowledging His goodness and power. As Paul wrote in Philippians 2:8, Jesus "humbled Himself and became obedient to the point of death, even the death of the cross." Jesus' choice of humility meant submitting to God's authority and His eternal plan to save us.

Jesus' willingness to submit to God's plan—"Thy will be done"—is an example to us (Matthew 26:42 KJV). It's another way of telling God we know His plan is best for us—that He is our Father and we are His trusting children. There is freedom and comfort in that surrender. Your strong Father cares for you, and He carries your burdens as you come to know your right place before Him.

Yes, humility is simple to understand, but it's not easy to live out. Yet God will enable you to humble yourself under His authority because He wants you to experience the freedom that comes with surrendering to Him.

God, show me the way of humility and
help me walk that path—by Your grace
and according to Your plan.

1 Peter 5:6–7

Humble yourselves under the *mighty* hand of God, that He may *exalt* you in due time, casting all your care upon Him, for He *cares* for you.

THE SHEPHERD'S ABUNDANCE

*I*f you're a devoted shepherd, guarding the sheep pen—especially at night—is essential because those who visit the pen under cover of darkness are up to no good. As Jesus put it, "The thief does not come except to steal, and to kill, and to destroy" (John 10:10). That doesn't just apply to sheep rustlers; it describes Satan today. This Enemy of God carefully schemes and slyly works to steal away from God the people He loves. Satan tries to convince us—as he convinced Eve in the garden—that God's way is not best for us, that He doesn't have our best interests at heart, and that taking charge of our own lives will lead to greater happiness and fulfillment.

Acting in sharp contrast to the sheep robber is the true shepherd who lays down his life to protect and provide for his sheep. Jesus, the Good Shepherd, has "come that [the sheep] may have life, and that they may have it more abundantly." The Son of our Creator understands why we were created, and He wants what is best for us. Abundant life comes when we walk closely with Him.

*Jesus, help me choose to walk in Your
ways and in close friendship with You
so that I may have abundant life.*

John 10:10

"I have come that they may have *life*, and that they may have it more *abundantly*."

INSEPARABLE

*F*eelings lie.

We may *feel* that God is far away and that He isn't hearing our prayers. We may *feel* ignored, forgotten, and unloved by Him. But, again, feelings don't necessarily correspond with reality. After all, they are influenced by a lack of sleep, a lack of food, or an abundance of hormones. Any grouchy or cheerful individual who crosses our path can influence our feelings and our mood.

Yes, feelings lie, and they can have a destructive ripple effect in a believer's life. So if you feel abandoned by God, panicked, or without God's love, don't give your feelings a foothold. When your emotions raise their voices, counter that noise with God's truth. Speak His Word out loud. Try it using today's verses from Romans 8. No matter how the Enemy protests, stand strong in God's truth. It may not take too many minutes or too many verses before the tide turns, feelings change, and you can again feel your Father's undying love for you.

Thank You, God, for never leaving me.
When my feelings try to take the wheel
of my life, give me power through Your
Word to steer it back toward You.

Romans 8:38–39

I am persuaded that neither death nor life, nor angels nor principalities nor powers, nor things present nor things to come, nor height nor depth, nor any other created thing, shall be able to separate us from the love of God which is in Christ Jesus our Lord.

BETTER TOGETHER

When God calls us to follow Jesus, He calls us to community. It's our natural habitat. We find it with others through things like regular church services, a small group, or a Bible study. Ideally, we have a little fun together too—eating meals, shopping, exercising, vacationing, and especially praying.

The writer of Hebrews knew that we need one another to spur us on to "love and good works." Yet it's tough to meet this standard. We think, *I'm busy. I'm more of a private person anyway.* And if we were honest, *It's easier to be anonymous at church than to connect* and *I don't like getting close to people.*

Of course, it's always easier to be anonymous. People tend to nudge us, bug us, and get under our skin. They expose our insecurities and occasionally put us out. But without them, we would not grow. God didn't put you on a desert island and tell you to fend for yourself. Instead, He planned for you a healthy, rich life in the company of His other children. Don't hide yourself away. Be a part of your faith family!

*God, teach me to be honest and genuine
in all of my relationships, and help me
learn from those You put in my life.*

Hebrews 10:24–25

Let us consider one another in order to stir up love and *good* works, not forsaking the *assembling* of ourselves together, as is the manner of some, but *exhorting* one another, and so much the more as you see the Day approaching.

EVEN IF HE DOESN'T

*T*hey had been warned. Shadrach, Meshach, and Abednego knew the consequences of not bowing before the golden statue of King Nebuchadnezzar: "Whoever does not fall down and worship shall be cast immediately into the midst of a burning fiery furnace" (Daniel 3:6).

Choosing to remain faithful to God, these three young men did not deny their disobedience when Nebuchadnezzar summoned them and gave them another chance to worship the statue. Instead, they boldly declared their confidence that God could save them from the fiery furnace—and then declared that they would not stop serving Him, *even if He didn't.*

"Even if He doesn't" faith recognizes God's authority and willingly submits to it. It trusts God even though the next step looks painful or dangerous, if not deadly. That kind of faith strengthens other believers and often piques the interest of nonbelievers.

What current situation in your life is an opportunity for "even if He doesn't" faith? As you pray, choose to remain faithful no matter what. And watch your Father work in your life and in those around you.

Lord, please grow in me loyalty and a faith that trusts Your plans for me are always best.

Daniel 3:17–18 NIV

If we are thrown into the blazing furnace, the God we serve is able to *deliver* us from it, and he will deliver us from Your Majesty's hand. But even if he does not, we want you to know, Your Majesty, that we will not *serve* your gods or *worship* the image of gold you have set up.

NOT IN VAIN

Steadfast. Immovable. Always abounding. It sounds like a tall order, doesn't it? We're mere mortals, after all, and we falter, move, and dry up in our faith from time to time. How could we possibly have the strength to "be steadfast, immovable, always abounding in the work of the Lord, knowing that [our] labor is not in vain in the Lord"? The answer is, it's not our strength; it's God's. He "gives us the victory through our Lord Jesus Christ" (1 Corinthians 15:57).

Oppression, peer pressure, chronic illness, persistent physical pain, broken relationships, pressing decisions, stress, exhaustion—so many things can weaken our stand in the Lord. We can too easily feel that following Jesus is futile (it can look awfully crazy to the world) and that our kingdom work is pointless (it tends not to bear the concrete, worldly, and satisfying fruit of power, possessions, and prestige).

When such feelings arise, look to Jesus' empty tomb. It helps us remember the big-picture perspective: Jesus rose from the dead and was victorious over sin, and He invites us into eternity with Him. Serving our glorious risen Lord will never be in vain.

Thank You, Jesus, for reminding me that I'm not alone on this earth. Help me to be steadfast and immovable in my faith.

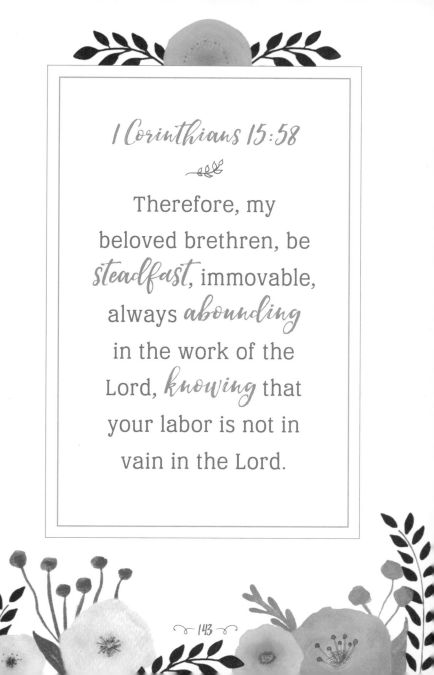

1 Corinthians 15:58

Therefore, my beloved brethren, be *steadfast*, immovable, always *abounding* in the work of the Lord, *knowing* that your labor is not in vain in the Lord.

YOUR REFUGE

*W*here do you go when life gets hard? Perhaps you take a walk, make a cup of tea, or turn on the TV to escape for just a minute. Thankfully, believers have somewhere even better to go when life gets hard: we can hide in the shadow of God's wings. We're like baby birds nestling in the feathers of a parent who provides food, protects, warms, and comforts. The key element that makes this refuge better than all others? He loves us.

This psalm refers to us as the apple of the Almighty's eye. What does that mean? One explanation is that the apple refers to the pupil of the human eye, so this expression means that the Lord protects you just as He would instinctively protect that vital organ of vision. Another explanation is that your loving God allows you to get close enough to Him that your image is reflected in the iris of His eye. In both explanations the bottom line is that God treasures you.

Whatever comes your way in the world, be confident that your heavenly Father will always offer you safety and love.

God, thank You for Your love and kindness and for providing me with a safe refuge. May I never hesitate to run to You when life is hard.

Psalm 17:7–8

Show Your marvelous
lovingkindness by Your
right hand, O You who
save those who *trust* in
You from those who
rise up against them.
Keep me as the apple
of Your eye; hide me
under the shadow
of Your *wings*.

THE JOYFUL RACE

The apostle Paul dearly loved the elders of the Ephesian church, and when he visited them on his way to Jerusalem, he wasn't sure if he would ever see them again. Before he prayed with them, Paul acknowledged the risks inherent in his trip to Jerusalem. All he knew, he reported, was that "chains and tribulations" awaited him (Acts 20:23).

Then he proclaimed that those dangers and risks were not going to keep him from going to Jerusalem. What mattered most to Paul was not how long his life lasted but that—however many days God gave him—he would "finish [his] race with joy" (v. 24).

Paul was confident that the Lord had called him to spread God's gospel, and he had faithfully fulfilled that calling, often at great cost to his physical health and safety. He had suffered for the sake of the gospel. And he was willing to suffer some more.

What an example for us! When life beats us down and we need to remind ourselves of what really matters, we can think of Paul and his commitment to Christ's gospel. Keep running, and keep your focus on God's eternal joy.

God, help me serve You with the kind
of commitment and focus Paul had so
I can finish the race with joy!

Acts 20:24

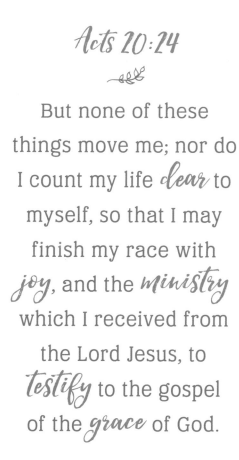

But none of these
things move me; nor do
I count my life *dear* to
myself, so that I may
finish my race with
joy, and the *ministry*
which I received from
the Lord Jesus, to
testify to the gospel
of the *grace* of God.

IN JESUS' NAME

Prayer is a privilege and, at times, a perplexing mystery. It's astounding that the Creator of the universe wants to talk with us. Yet when He doesn't answer our prayers as we think He should, we can get discouraged. Some say that in those situations God is answering with either a "no" or a "not yet." But when we're asking for something that seems like His will—saving a soul, healing a marriage—why would He wait? The truth is, we may not know this side of heaven. But we can know He has a plan, and He listens when we pray.

One important teaching about prayer is Jesus' instruction to pray to God in His name. The promise in today's verse is not a magic trick, just as God Himself is not some genie in a bottle, waiting to grant us whatever we request. When we pray in the name *Jesus*, however, we remember that we can approach God only because of Jesus' sacrifice. We also remember that God is God, and we're not. So when you pray in Jesus' name, acknowledge what He has done out of love for you, and have faith that God operates in ways far greater than we can understand.

*Lord, make me a person who prays
passionately, regularly, confidently,
and always in the name of Jesus.*

John 16:23

"Most assuredly,
I say to you,
whatever you *ask* the
Father in My name
He will *give* you."

EVERYDAY FAITH

*F*ace it. Doing laundry and getting the oil changed are simply not glamorous activities. Washing dishes, changing diapers, and clocking in for a nine-to-five job are not at all glitzy. Yet any of these mundane tasks is redeemed and made significant when we do each one *with* and *for* the Lord.

That's the wisdom of Colossians 3:23: "Whatever you do, do your work heartily, as for the Lord rather than for men" (NASB).

What would it be like to drive the carpool, run the department, volunteer in the classroom, or make rounds at the hospital with a keen awareness of God's presence? Imagine that Christ is standing right beside you as you work, remaining with you through the tedium or the difficulty. He gave you this work to do, and His love will carry you through. So pray to Him in your ordinary, day-to-day tasks, no matter how mundane. Remember that when you are in conversation with the One who loves you and who gives you life, even the dullest work can become worship.

God, teach me to walk through each day very
aware that You are with me, and help me
to be in constant conversation with You.

Colossians 3:23 NASB

Whatever you do,
do your work
heartily, as for
the Lord rather
than for men.

BLESS THE LORD

*W*hat concerns are weighing most heavily on your heart right now? Maybe you just learned that your friend's cancer has returned—again. Or your child is dealing with the consequences of a poor moral decision. Perhaps your elderly mother is not pleased that you are taking away her driver's license.

Of course, all life's concerns call for prayer. We fall at the Lord's feet, not necessarily understanding why He has allowed what He has allowed or why He seems so distant. We pray as best we can, and we let others pray for us. We just keep putting one foot in front of the other.

Job certainly suffered, yet he was determined to keep worshipping the Lord through painful events. His story reminds us that God doesn't always behave the way we expect Him to. Nor does He always act when we think it would be the perfect time for Him to intervene. And, as Job himself would testify, He doesn't always protect us from loss and pain. But we must continue to bless Him.

In those dark times when the Lord "has taken away," may we choose—as Job himself did—to bless the Lord with determination.

Lord, teach me to accept from Your hand the hard and the easy times—and to do so graciously.

Job 1:21

Naked I came from my mother's *womb*, and naked shall I return there. The LORD gave, and the LORD has taken away; *blessed* be the name of the LORD.

ACCEPTING GRACE

*J*ust show me what to do! Point me in the right direction! How high do you want me to jump? What boxes do I have to check off? We may not always like the results of systems like these, but at least they make sense to us. Consequences always match our actions, for better or worse.

God's economy is very different. Oh, He points us in the right direction: He gave us His law as well as the example of His Son, who lived out that law perfectly. But for us, the law showed us how far short of God's standards we fall. We also learned that there is nothing we can do to get rid of that sinfulness—at least, nothing we can do on our own.

Enter God's grace! Salvation from sin and its consequences—death and eternal separation from God—is His gift of grace to us. And that can be unsettling, because we so often feel we have to earn good things. But God's grace is a free gift that cannot be earned. Choose today to make your life an everyday journey of accepting, not earning, this amazing grace.

God, thank You for Your free gift of grace. Help me accept Your grace and then share it with others so they can know You and Your love.

Titus 2:11

The *grace* of God that brings *salvation* has appeared to all men.

BE A LIGHT

*Y*ou are the light of the world."

Think of a candle lit in a dark corner. That's us. God placed us in our neighborhoods, schools, workplaces, and activities to be His light. People in the dark—spiritually, emotionally, or psychologically—need light to find their way out. As God's people, we can light the path out of darkness, toward the hope and wholeness Jesus offers.

But we can't do this if we hide that light of Christ within us. Whether it's nervousness, lack of confidence, or fear of rejection, if we let feelings like these—planted by the Enemy—affect our behavior and keep us from sharing Christ, we may be hiding our light. But as Christians, we are not meant to be hidden; we are meant to shine God's light for all to see.

That's why Jesus makes His command crystal clear: "Let your light so shine before men, that they may see your good works and glorify your Father in heaven" (Matthew 5:16). How can you let your light shine where you are today?

Lord, I don't want anything to hinder me from shining for You. Make Your light bright in me.

Matthew 5:14–15

"You are the *light* of the world. A city that is set on a hill cannot be *hidden*. Nor do they light a lamp and put it under a basket, but on a lampstand, and it *gives* light to all who are in the house."

CHOOSE CONTENTMENT

*I*s your glass half empty or half full? Whatever bent your personality naturally takes, you do have a choice in your outlook on life. Maybe those with half-full glasses among us don't need the lesson Paul talked about in Philippians 4, but listen up, empties! You may be melancholy by nature: that's how God made you, you say. That doesn't mean you can't learn contentment.

Yes, the world has come a long way—all of it downhill—since Eden. Yes, the human race is living with wrong priorities. But you know the author of history! You know who wins in the end!

Paul learned to be content whatever his circumstances, and he knew very difficult circumstances (2 Corinthians 11:23–27). Perhaps knowing that Jesus is indeed the ultimate Victor helped Paul. Or maybe he chose to focus on the truth that nothing could separate him from God's love. Or perhaps he experienced the Spirit's peace that surpasses understanding, so contentment was an easy choice.

Cling to these truths through every difficulty, and learn to choose contentment.

God, help me choose contentment, whatever my circumstances, confident of Your sovereignty, Your victory, and Your unfailing love for me.

Philippians 4:11

I have *learned*
in whatever
state I am,
to be *content*.

A PERSONAL STORY

*W*hen the fullness of time had come . . ." It sounds like the start of a storybook, doesn't it? For many of us, this story feels oh-so familiar, like a cherished children's book we could recite almost in our sleep.

But the story of Jesus' birth is not just a story! It's a revolutionary truth. Look at today's verse not as a familiar tale, but as a breaking news report. Notice the wondrous truths that you may have heard hundreds of times. God's Son was "born of a woman." We are adopted as sons, and we receive His Spirit. We are privileged to call the almighty Creator "Abba, Father." And we receive these blessings—and many others—through Christ who died as payment for our sins.

When you change the way you hear this story, how might that change the way you tell it? Do you know what you would say to someone who wants to know the reason for the hope within you (1 Peter 3:15)? God gave you a story to tell, and it's deeply personal and individual. By the power of the Holy Spirit within you, your own story will make the truths of Galatians 4 come alive.

God, bring Your story to life within me,
and show me how to share it.

Galatians 4:4–7

When the fullness of the time had come, God sent forth His Son, born of a woman, born under the law, to *redeem* those who were under the law, that we might *receive* the adoption as sons. And because you are sons, God has sent forth the Spirit of His Son into your *hearts*, crying out, "Abba, Father!" Therefore you are no longer a slave but a son, and if a son, then an heir of God through *Christ*.

WORTHY OF WORSHIP

*T*he setting is the throne room of heaven. A rainbow encircles the throne, and sitting on it is One who "was like a jasper and a sardius stone in appearance" (Revelation 4:3)—that is, shining like a blindingly bright gemstone. Twenty-four elders, each on a throne, are wearing radiant white robes and golden crowns. Thunder and lightning come forth from the throne, and seven lamps of fire burn in front of it.

Four mysterious living creatures—resembling a lion, a calf, a man, and a flying eagle—sing their own song of worship: "Holy, holy, holy, Lord God Almighty, who was and is and is to come!" (v. 8). Their words resound in the throne room, declaring the worthiness of the sovereign Holy One. He created all things, He sustains His creation, and He alone deserves glory, honor, and power.

Revelation 4 offers a scene in the future, but even the world we live in now has its own ways of inspiring adoration and worship. Where can you find hints of God's majesty? What reveals to you something of His infinite power? And what does your song of praise sound like? The Lord truly is worthy of all your praise!

You created us to praise You, God. And
You alone are worthy of praise!

Revelation 4:11

You are worthy, O Lord,

to receive glory and

honor and *power*; for

You created all things,

and by Your will they

exist and were created.

TAKE CARE OF THE TEMPLE

E at this! Wear this! Work out this long and this often! Take this supplement! We can get lots of input from many sources about how to take care of our bodies. In 1 Corinthians 6:19, though, the apostle Paul set forth the solid bottom line for each one of us.

Your body is "the temple of the Holy Spirit," he wrote. Paul was telling believers that our bodies are a sanctuary for God, where His glory resides.

Think about that for a minute. The all-holy, almighty God has chosen to take up residence within you to guide you, grow you, and bless you. What are the implications of this in your life? Consider specifically which behaviors or attitudes affect your health and body. What activities should you stop doing, and what activities should you start doing? Which of your attitudes have been harmful to yourself and others? How do you dress your temple? And are you exercising enough? What about your diet?

Care for your body, for your own sake and because it is the dwelling place of God.

You, Lord, deserve the best of dwelling places. Help me strive for a healthy body so I can honor Your presence within me every moment of my life.

1 Corinthians 6:19

Do you not know that your *body* is the *temple* of the Holy Spirit who is in you, whom you have from *God*, and you are not your own?

HEALING CONFESSION

*Y*ou've probably heard it said that confession is good for the soul. Perhaps you've even experienced the relief yourself in prayer. God is always faithful to forgive you when you acknowledge your sin before Him (1 John 1:9). Or maybe you've also experienced something similar after confessing a sin to a trusted fellow believer (James 5:16)—and the response was a taste of God's unconditional love for you. Confession promotes healing of our relationship with God and of our soul.

Sometimes, though, we are so comfortable with a particular behavior or attitude that we don't recognize it as sin. This reality prompted David's prayer in Psalm 139:23–24. He wanted to identify sin and seek its remedy so he could be closer to God.

The act of confession itself is not a cure-all, though it does ease the burden from our soul. The actual remedy for our sin was Jesus' death: He died in our place so that we could be righteous and forgiven in God's sight.

So regularly confess your sin, and when you do, look at the cross. Jesus went there to provide a remedy for all our sin.

Holy Spirit, please work in my heart
to reveal my sin so I can confess and
fully accept God's forgiveness.

Psalm 139:23-24

Search me, O God, and know my heart; try me, and know my anxieties; and see if there is any wicked way in me, and lead me in the way everlasting.

HIGHER WAYS

*T*ornadoes uproot houses, and earthquakes crumble buildings. Hurricanes flood acres of land, and tsunamis wipe towns off the map. Disease takes victims of all ages. Families, marriages, and hearts are broken. Any one of these facts of life—and there are many others—are reasons people give for not believing in God. Who wants anything to do with a God who allows such pain?

These realities make even believers scratch their heads. Oh, we know that Jesus warns that we'll have trials and tribulations in this world—but why do children have to suffer because of someone else's sin? And why are devoted Christians among the dead when a natural disaster strikes?

We don't understand God. We don't know what He is thinking, and neither did Isaiah thousands of years ago. But we do know that He is good—always. Even when things don't make sense or when life hands us tragedy. His ways are higher, and one day we will see this for ourselves in His presence. So let us offer our pain to Him who suffered pain for us—to Jesus. Turn yourself over to His mysterious ways, and see how He can bring strength and healing.

God, Your ways are beyond my ability
to understand, yet You are so good.
Help me to turn to You in my pain.

Isaiah 55:8–9

"For My thoughts are not your *thoughts*, nor are your ways My ways," says the LORD. "For as the *heavens* are higher than the earth, so are My ways *higher* than your ways, and My thoughts than your thoughts."

THE FULLNESS

*W*e've all done it. We've made an assumption about something and clung to it as truth. Maybe a coworker was a little curt to you one morning, and now you *know* he dislikes you. Or perhaps a supervisor didn't comment on your big presentation, so you just *know* she wasn't impressed. When we make the leap from assumption to belief without using truth as a foundation, our perceptions of life are not necessarily a true reflection of reality. And these kinds of misunderstandings will only lead to even more misunderstandings—and that's a mess that no one wants to be in.

Thankfully, we don't have to guess how God feels about us. No matter if we *think* God is distant or *feel* like He is unconcerned about us, we can read Ephesians 3:17–19 to hear the truth—that God's love for us is wide and long and deep and high. In fact, God's love is so big, it surpasses all understanding!

Whenever we spend time with the Lord, we begin to understand His love for us a little better than we did before. And as we grow in our understanding of His love, we are "filled with all the fullness of God." That fullness will keep us grounded in His love and truth so we can live by faith in Him and not by our own assumptions.

Lord, help me to be grounded in Your love and truth.

Ephesians 3:17–19

May [Christ] *dwell* in your hearts through *faith*; that you, being rooted and grounded in love, may be able to comprehend with all the *saints* what is the width and length and depth and height—to know the *love* of Christ which passes *knowledge*; that you may be filled with all the *fullness* of God.

LIVING SACRIFICES

What Bible scenes do you think of when you hear the word *sacrifice*? Maybe it's the Genesis 22 account of Abraham and Isaac. God commanded Abraham to sacrifice his long-awaited firstborn son, through whom God had promised to bless the world. Amazingly, Abraham obeyed without hesitation—and God provided a replacement sacrifice just moments before Abraham was to kill his only son.

Then there are the New Testament accounts of Jesus' sacrifice on the cross, but this time God did not provide a replacement. He allowed His only Son to suffer for our sins—and Jesus submitted to that plan.

Then Paul wrote that we are to "offer [our] bodies as a living sacrifice." We are to die to self—to our sinful desires, to our own will, and to dreams that are not in line with God's plans. How do we do that? We obey His commands rather than let the world shape us. We submit to God's will in all we do, just as Jesus did. But ours is not a one-time act. We must die to self every day. And every time we bring ourselves back to that altar, we become more alive in Him.

Lord, I know that life works better
when I live it according to Your will.
Please help me do exactly that.

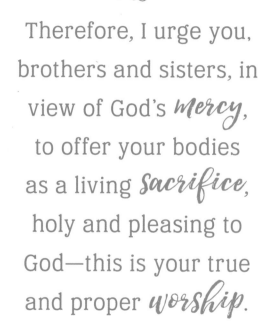

Romans 12:1 NIV

Therefore, I urge you, brothers and sisters, in view of God's *mercy*, to offer your bodies as a living *sacrifice*, holy and pleasing to God—this is your true and proper *worship*.

LESSONS LEARNED

*N*ear the close of David's reign, he did what many dads would do: he passed the baton to one of his sons. But before handing over the scepter to Solomon, David had a few thoughts to share. After all, David knew the demands, the pressures, the temptations, and the responsibilities of the kingship. And he had learned some life lessons the hard way.

David had often sought the Lord for guidance and direction. Having hidden God's Word in his heart, David knew God's commands and obeyed them. At times, though, he had gone his own way—and paid the price. But after David sinned, he confessed and eloquently celebrated God's forgiveness (Psalm 51).

David understood the importance of knowing God, of serving Him with a loyal heart and a willing mind, and of seeking Him persistently. David also knew that forsaking God comes with a huge cost. And he wanted to pass these lessons along to his son.

Father knows best, but will we listen? May we learn from these lessons what David learned the hard way!

Help me, Lord, to learn from what David told Solomon and never forsake You.

1 Chronicles 28:9

As for you, my son Solomon, know the God of your father, and *serve* Him with a loyal heart and with a willing mind; for the Lord searches all *hearts* and *understands* all the intent of the thoughts. If you *seek* Him, He will be found by you; but if you *forsake* Him, He will cast you off forever.

UNFAILING GOD

*I*f you've read the news or turned on the TV lately, you know the world can be a scary and dangerous place. How do parents even let children out into that frightening world if they aren't entrusting them to the Lord's care? "Hope it all works out for you" seems a little weak, and "Just have faith!" seems to be an incomplete instruction.

How could we possibly trust God in this world? We know He is the designer of the universe, the author of history, and the Victor over sin and death. This all-powerful God, however, is not some distant, impersonal force. Instead, He knows your name, your heart, and your tears. He is merciful, compassionate, and faithful.

In God alone we find genuine hope for the circumstances of the world and the future of our kids. Hope that is not rooted in Him is really just wishful thinking, and faith in anything or anyone else is baseless.

No matter what happens, no matter what our world looks like, we can know that God takes care of us. His mercies are new every morning.

Teach me, Father, to rest in Your loving faithfulness, to keep my eyes on Jesus, and to put my hope in Him alone.

Lamentations 3:22–23

Through the LORD's *mercies* we are not consumed, because His *compassions* fail not. They are new every morning; great is Your *faithfulness*.

LOVE WITH GOD'S LOVE

*I*t's a basic law of physics: for every action there is an equal and opposite reaction. This principle seems to function in human relationships too. One mean word prompts another mean word. One selfish act invites another in return. One nasty look receives a glare in response. We simply react!

It's easy to just react instead of thinking about our responses to people—whether they are kind or mean. Even if we try to think before we speak and not retaliate when someone hurts us, taking an eye for an eye comes much easier than turning the other cheek.

That's why we need the Holy Spirit. The Spirit's work in our hearts bears the fruit of "love, joy, peace, longsuffering, kindness, goodness, faithfulness, gentleness, [and] self-control" (Galatians 5:22–23). This fruit of transformation will help us do a better job of returning a kind word for a mean one, an unselfish act for a selfish one, and a look of compassion for a glare. In other words, the Spirit will enable us to treat others the way we ourselves want to be treated. Let's invite Him into our everyday interactions so we can demonstrate God's love.

Holy Spirit, please continue Your transforming work in me. Show me how to love with God's love.

Matthew 7:12

"Whatever you want men to do to you, do *also* to them, for this is the *law* and the Prophets."

GOD WRITES OUR DAYS

*T*hink about all the hats you wear: spouse, parent, volunteer, employee, neighbor, chef, gardener, chauffeur, handy-person, homework consultant, dog walker, and undoubtedly many others.

In all the things we're in charge of, we like to maintain an illusion of control. That illusion, however, can easily be shattered by a traffic accident, an illness, a job layoff, or other countless, unexpected twists in the road. When we encounter those twists, we do well to remember that our sovereign God is not surprised; He is never surprised by the course our life takes.

Clearly David found comfort in this truth. Meditating on God's hand in his life, he reminded himself in this psalm that, even before he was born, "all [his days] were written, the days fashioned for [him]" by the almighty God. Nothing that happens to us is an accident. No event is beyond God's ability to deliver or redeem. And, by God's grace, no pain or loss will be for naught. So rest in God's sovereignty. Find peace in the fact that your chaotic life is actually under His perfect control.

Lord, when chaos comes, may I rest
in You, knowing that all my days have
long been written in Your book.

Psalm 139:16

Your eyes saw my *substance*, being yet unformed. And in Your *book* they all were written, the days *fashioned* for me, when as yet there were none of them.

WORK IN PROGRESS

*D*o you sometimes have a difficult time finishing a project you start? Are you easily discouraged if you encounter unanticipated roadblocks? And what if you are part of a team and some members seem to take the project two steps backward every time they try to help? Fortunately, our heavenly Father is not like that at all.

Even if we're rough material for God to work with, He won't stop renewing us until He finishes. And He won't consider Himself finished until the final product meets His high standards of purity and holiness and we are made like Christ. He is not surprised if we resist with hardened hearts or hectic schedules. He knows we'll make wrong choices and have wrong priorities. Yet God will not let us go.

Think about it: He knows every thought you've had, every word you've said, and everything you've done, and He *still* claims you as His own. He will clean you up and make you new until you are the creation He made you to be.

Yes, you were made by the Master Artist, and the One who began that good work in you will indeed see it through to completion.

God, help me open my heart to Your life-changing love. Thank You for renewing me for Your glory!

Philippians 1:6

Being *confident* of this very thing, that He who has begun a good work in you will *complete* it until the day of Jesus Christ.

LIGHT BURDENS

Paul does a good job here of making a surprising case: that heavy is light. It's all a matter of perspective.

A burden is heavy when its presence is pointless, when traveling with it is lonely, and when the journey is long. Yet Paul reminds us that life's afflictions are purposeful, not pointless. God uses our hardships to make us more like Jesus, and no purpose is greater than that.

And we need not travel alone during this lifelong process of transformation. Fellow believers have their own afflictions too, and we can be reminders for one another that hard times come—but that God is sovereign over even those hard times. Plus, companionship makes a hard journey seem shorter. Others' support can also help us keep focused not on the struggles but on the unseen and eternal rewards that God has for His people.

No pain is wasted in God's economy as He works to transform us. And no hardship needs to be endured alone. Trust in God's sovereign goodness, walk with His people, and remind yourself that the unseen and eternal are far more important than the seen and temporary. Life's afflictions will then seem lighter.

Thank You for putting my life into perspective.
Help me choose the eternal over the temporary.

2 Corinthians 4:16–18

Therefore we do not lose *heart*. Even though our outward man is perishing, yet the inward man is being *renewed* day by day. For our light affliction, which is but for a moment, is working for us a far more exceeding and eternal weight of *glory*, while we do not look at the things which are seen, but at the things which are not seen. For the things which are seen are temporary, but the things which are not seen are *eternal*.

A SURE THING

*W*hat are you hoping for? Probably not winning the lottery. You know the odds are very much against you. You probably don't hope that Prince Charming will knock on your door. You know that only happens in fairy tales. And you're probably not hoping for a cure for the common cold to be announced anytime soon. You know that scientists have been trying to nail that virus for years.

In the eighteenth century Alexander Pope noted that "hope springs eternal in the human breast." That may be so, but whatever we are hoping for will determine whether or not our hope will pay off. Sure, we can hope that we hit the jackpot. But wouldn't our hope be better placed in a sure thing?

Christ is our sure thing. When we give ourselves to Him, we know He will walk with us and guide us. We have faith, even in the tough times, because we are sure of what we hope for and certain of what we can't see: our eternal life with Him.

Hope in anything or anyone other than the Lord may disappoint. Hope that the Lord will bless a life of faith in Him will never disappoint.

Lord, thank You for the very
real hope I have in You.

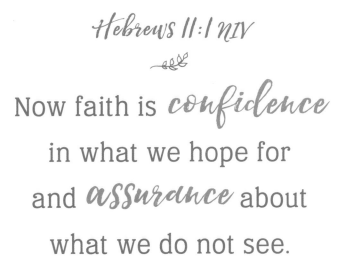

Hebrews 11:1 NIV

Now faith is *confidence*
in what we hope for
and *assurance* about
what we do not see.

FIND REST IN JESUS

*I*f you're a parent, don't you wish you could sometimes be sent to timeout? To go to your room for twenty minutes? To sit quietly in the corner and think about what just happened? Aaaahhhh . . .

Well, that's the kind of invitation Jesus has extended to you. He invites you to go to Him and receive some much-needed soul rest.

Consider what burdens are weighing you down. Perhaps it's sin, overwork, or loneliness. Maybe yours is the burden of anxiety, depression, fear, or doubt. The alternative to these burdens is the yoke Jesus offers. An ox wears a yoke to attach it to a plow so the farmer can steer it. And like an ox, if we are to put on the yoke our Lord has custom-made for us, we have to take off any other yokes that are currently weighing us down.

Taking on the yoke of Christ is choosing to obey His Word and to be guided by Him. And when we take it on, He promises that we will "find rest."

The rest Jesus promises is rooted in God's love for us. So come to Him, and find rest for your soul.

Father, I choose Your yoke. Thank
You for giving me rest.

Matthew 11:28–30

"Come to Me, all you who
labor and are heavy laden,
and I will give you *rest*.
Take My yoke upon you
and learn from Me,
for I am *gentle* and lowly
in *heart*, and you will
find rest for your souls.
For My yoke is *easy* and
My burden is light."

A WAY OUT

*M*aybe you've said with a wry smile, "God won't let us be tempted beyond what we can handle—but I think He has me confused with someone else!"

Every one of us knows that feeling. We are all well aware of the many temptations that fill our world and often fill our days.

During their forty-year journey between Egypt and Canaan, God's people misused their freedom and were tripped up by prideful overconfidence. The behavior that resulted included idolatry, sexual immorality, rebelliousness, testing God, complaining—and we could easily be guilty of the same, if we haven't been already.

So let's learn from our ancestors in the faith. God is faithful to help us stand strong in the face of temptation. He will not give us an impossible-to-resist temptation, and He will always provide a way of escape. We do, however, need to be willing to humbly cry out to Him for help.

If there's a verse worth hiding in your heart, it's 1 Corinthians 10:13. Its rich truth will help you live out your faith when temptation strikes—and to live it out for your good and for God's glory.

Lord, remind me to cry out to You whenever I face temptation and need Your strength and protection.

1 Corinthians 10:13

No temptation has *overtaken* you except such as is common to man; but God is *faithful*, who will not allow you to be tempted beyond what you are able, but with the *temptation* will also make the way of escape, that you may be able to *bear* it.

MUSTARD SEEDS AND MOUNTAINS

*I*t's an old hiking trick that applies to our faith walk as well: don't look too far ahead. If the path ahead is rugged and steep, barren and dusty, or stretching out to who knows where, the view of the distance can discourage you from going any farther. The prospect of what lies ahead can sap you of energy and enthusiasm and kill any desire to move ahead.

Life with the Lord is a journey, and sometimes the trail ahead can be less than inviting. The terrain can be hostile and the circumstances impassable. Perhaps your life's mountain is too steep and rugged, especially for someone with your limited climbing experience. And, yes, by now your feet might be blistered and sore.

When you come to such a point in your faith journey, Jesus calls you to trust Him, but He doesn't require a lot of trust. Jesus calls for faith the size of a mustard seed, and that would be about 1/20 of an inch. That's pretty small—especially next to a mountain. But He'll take your tiny seed of faith and use it beyond anything you could ever imagine!

*Lord Jesus, thank You that my mustard-
seed faith won't keep You from
handling the mountains in my life.*

Matthew 17:20

"If you have *faith* as a mustard seed, you will say to this *mountain*, 'Move from here to there,' and it will move; and nothing will be *impossible* for you."

193

OUR NEVER-DISTANT GOD

*G*azing at majestic mountain peaks, listening to crashing thunder, seeing the ocean roll—moments like these remind us of the otherness of our eternal, omnipresent, and infinitely powerful God. He deserves our respect and awe that compel us to fall down before Him. To Him, as Jude declared, "be glory and majesty, dominion and power, both now and forever. Amen."

Sometimes in our mind, God seems to be the gentle grandfather, the buddy and friend, or the generous Santa Claus in the sky. We do a great disservice to ourselves and our relationship with our heavenly Father when we lose sight of His awesome otherness. But we don't want to gain that perspective and, at the same time, lose our awareness that He is our personal Savior, Redeemer, heavenly Father, and constant companion through life.

No matter how unfathomable He is, He makes Himself accessible to us. He bends down so we can come close to Him. He makes the world turn on its axis, but He still holds our hands to keep us from stumbling. What an amazing mystery! He certainly deserves glory, now and forever. Amen!

Thank You, God, for showing me
both Your immeasurable power and
Your personal love and care.

Jude vv. 24–25

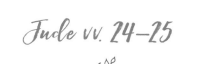

Now to Him who is able to
keep you from *stumbling*,
and to present you faultless
before the presence of
His *glory* with exceeding
joy, to God our Savior, who
alone is wise, be glory
and *majesty*, dominion
and power, both now
and forever. Amen.

GOOD PLANS

*T*here's nothing like a flashlight when the power goes out. There's nothing like a hug when the world seems to have turned against you. And there's nothing like good news when the future looks bleak. Today's passage was something like that for the Jews who were still being held captive in Babylon.

Speaking to His suffering people, God made promises about what would happen once their exile in Babylon was over. He told the struggling people of Israel that He had good plans for them and that they could trust Him to provide them with a wonderful future. Their relationship with Him would be fully restored.

Maybe you feel as if you're in a Babylon of your own. Consequences from past decisions are weighing you down, you feel captive to hardships in the present, and you see only darkness ahead. If any of that applies to you, accept God's invitation to you. He will hear your prayers, He will be found by you when you seek Him, and He has wonderful plans for your future.

Move on from past mistakes and missteps. Choose to walk with your Lord today. And look to the future, trusting your good God and the plans He has custom-made for you.

God, I praise You that Your plans for me
are full of Your mercy, grace, and love.

Jeremiah 29:11–13 NIV

"For I know the plans I have for you," declares the Lord, "plans to *prosper* you and not to harm you, plans to give you *hope* and a future. Then you will call on me and come and *pray* to me, and I will listen to you. You will *seek* me and find me when you seek me with all your heart."

PSALM OF ASCENT

Psalm 121—one of the fifteen songs or psalms of ascent—was a marching song for faithful Jews making their way to Jerusalem for one of the three yearly feasts. With Jerusalem at an elevation of about 2,700 feet, the ascent was literal, but today this psalm still helps worshippers ascend figuratively into the presence of the Lord—our keeper, our shade, the preserver of our souls, and our protector along the journey of life.

Reflect for a few minutes on times when you have been very aware of God acting in your life in one or two of the ways these lines describe. When, for instance, has God been your keeper or your shade? When has He clearly preserved you from the evil that flourishes in this fallen world?

As you walk this leg of your life journey, are there times when you feel as if you're truly climbing a mountain? In what ways do you need your Lord to be your shade? From what evil would you like Him to protect you? Know that your heavenly Father is up to the task. An ever-vigilant shepherd, He never slumbers or sleeps.

*Thank You for the gift of a memory, Lord, so that
I can recall Your great faithfulness to me. Keep
me mindful of Your companionship in my life.*

Psalm 121:1–2, 5–8

I will lift up my eyes to the hills—
from whence comes my help? My
help comes from the LORD, who
made *heaven* and *earth*. . . . The
LORD is your keeper; the LORD is
your shade at your right hand. The
sun shall not strike you by day,
nor the moon by night. The LORD
shall preserve you from all evil;
He shall preserve your soul. The
LORD shall preserve your going out
and your coming in from this time
forth, and even *forevermore*.

GIVER OF STRENGTH

*S*hipwrecked, beaten, imprisoned, stoned, run out of town, hungry, thirsty, cold, naked, threatened by Gentiles and fellow Jews, facing danger in cities, on the sea, and in the wilderness—Paul experienced all of this and more as he served Jesus. And who saw him through? Jesus. Each step of the way. God didn't just say He would see Paul through; He showed it.

What are you facing right now? Perhaps you're dealing with a shipwrecked relationship or a taking a beating in your place of employment. Maybe you feel imprisoned by past sin, unpaid bills, or a meaningless job. You may be fighting loneliness or isolation. Life can be very difficult, but hear again the confident statement of the apostle Paul: "I can do everything through Christ, who gives me strength."

Jesus is an unwavering source of strength for us, the most reliable source available to us. He will never leave you or forsake you (Hebrews 13:5). He will show Himself to be sufficient to meet your every need. Turn to Him, and give Him the opportunity to do just that.

God, how will I know You to be sufficient to meet my every need if I don't turn to You in the midst of them? Please enable me to trust You more.

Philippians 4:13 NLT

For I can do
everything through
Christ, who gives
me *strength*.

OUR FATHER . . .

*E*ntire books have been written about the Lord's Prayer and complete chapters about a single line. And that isn't too surprising. After all, this example is given to us by the One who lived a life of constant connection to the Father.

As familiar as this prayer may be to you, try to imagine how radical the first two words—"Our Father"—must have sounded to Jewish ears in the first century. For generations the Almighty's name had been too holy to say out loud. But Jesus encouraged all believers to make a drastic shift and approach their King as their heavenly Father. The holy God of Israel welcomes us just like an earthly father drawing his kids into a warm embrace.

But consider what we learn about this Father at the end of the prayer. Jesus' words point to the majesty and otherness of our God: "For Yours is the kingdom and the power and the glory forever." Our warm, caring, heavenly Father is at the same time the infinitely powerful King of all creation. And we are privileged to crawl onto His lap and share our hearts.

God, what a blessing and a privilege to be Your child—and to know that Your kingdom, power, and glory are forever!

Matthew 6:9–13

"Our Father in heaven, hallowed be Your name. Your kingdom come. Your will be done on earth as it is in *heaven*. Give us this day our daily bread. And *forgive* us our debts, as we forgive our debtors. And do not lead us into temptation, but deliver us from the evil one. For Yours is the kingdom and the power and the *glory* forever. Amen."

SHOUT TO THE LORD!

*I*t's a command made easy to follow. Psalm 100 opens with the call to joyfully praise the Lord and then offers several reasons why we should do exactly that.

God is like a shepherd who protects and provides for His helpless sheep. It's not a flattering description, but like sheep, we find ourselves drawn to unhealthy waters. Sometimes we get ourselves turned upside down and can't get right side up without the Shepherd's help.

Our God is good. He wants what is best for us, and He especially desires to have us walk with Him closely every day of our lives.

In sharp contrast to human love that can be fickle, God's love will last forever. He won't change His mind; He won't find someone better to love. And there's nothing you can do to make Him love you less or more.

God has been faithful to generations before us, He shows Himself faithful to us, and He will be faithful to every generation to come. Clearly, we have no reason not to obey the Psalm 100 command! Let us worship the Lord with gladness and joyful songs!

Lord, I praise You because You are good, I am Yours, and Your faithfulness will continue forever.

Psalm 100:1–3 NIV

Shout for joy to the LORD,
all the earth. Worship the
LORD with *gladness*; come
before him with *joyful* songs.
Know that the LORD is God. It
is he who made us, and we
are his; we are his people,
the *sheep* of his *pasture*.

MY FAVORITE
BIBLE VERSES

_____

_____

_____

_____

_____

_____

_____